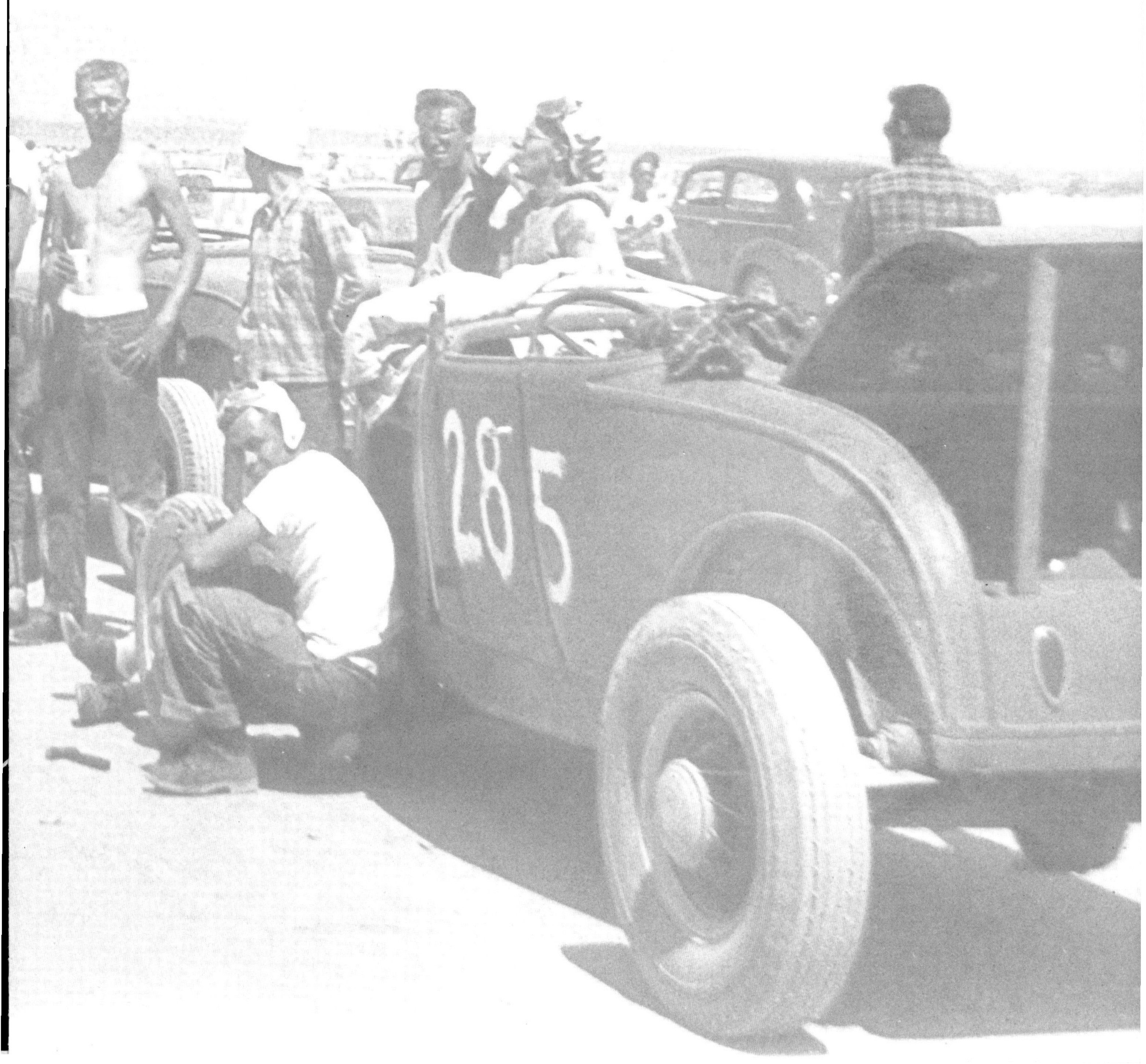
285

To Mark & Wendy
Enjoy the pics!
Best, Art Ganahl
'14

Hot Rod Gallery

by Pat Ganahl

A Nostalgic
Look at Hot Rodding's
Golden Years: 1930-1960

CarTech®

CarTech®, Inc.
39966 Grand Avenue
North Branch, MN 55056
Phone: 651-277-1200 or 800-551-4754
Fax: 651-277-1203
www.cartechbooks.com

© 2014 by Pat Ganahl

All rights reserved. No part of this publication may be reproduced or utilized in any form or by any means, electronic or mechanical, including photocopying, recording, or by any information storage and retrieval system, without prior permission from the Publisher. All text, photographs, and artwork are the property of the Author unless otherwise noted or credited.

The information in this work is true and complete to the best of our knowledge. However, all information is presented without any guarantee on the part of the Author or Publisher, who also disclaim any liability incurred in connection with the use of the information and any implied warranties of merchantability or fitness for a particular purpose. Readers are responsible for taking suitable and appropriate safety measures when performing any of the operations or activities described in this work.

All trademarks, trade names, model names and numbers, and other product designations referred to herein are the property of their respective owners and are used solely for identification purposes. This work is a publication of CarTech, Inc., and has not been licensed, approved, sponsored, or endorsed by any other person or entity. The Publisher is not associated with any product, service, or vendor mentioned in this book, and does not endorse the products or services of any vendor mentioned in this book.

Edit by Bob Wilson
Layout by Monica Seiberlich
Design concept by Connie DeFlorin

ISBN 978-1-61325-115-7
Item No. CT523

Library of Congress Cataloging-in-Publication Data Available

Written, edited, and designed in the U.S.A.
Printed in China
10 9 8 7 6 5 4 3 2 1

Front Flap: This is the famous "long black line" at Bonneville, that the race cars followed, as far and as fast as possible, toward the "floating mountain" looming just over the all-white horizon. You can't experience it unless you're there, but this photo gives a hint.

Frontispiece: It's a good year at Bonneville, weather-wise, because the rock-hard salt has been blackened by dozens of cars making hundreds of runs. This show-quality 1927 T street roadster has come all the way from Indiana to try its best running the black line.

Title Page: Young Don Van Hoff built this chopped, four-carb flathead-powered Deuce five-window while he was in high school, even keeping it a secret from his dad. The color in this image reflects the colors used when it ran on the December 1955 HRM Cover.

Table of Contents: Just one year after the Outlaw, Roth trumped himself with the bubble-topped Beatnik Bandit. To give a small idea of the "Wow!" factor of these cars at the time, mega-promoter Bob Larivee bought both cars and featured them at all his shows across the country. Revell sold millions of models of them. Roth built them so he could dazzle young kids at shows and sell them T-shirts, decals, and other trinkets . . . and he did it quite successfully.

Back Cover Photos

Top: Junior climbed onto a nearby roof to get this high-angle color photo of a one-day parking lot show "At the Sears in Compton in 1956." It must be late 1956, because there are few new 1957 cars. Of note in the foreground is a tri-power V-8 red 1954 Corvette, Bruce Giesler's pink (ex-Ayala) GMC pickup, and what Junior thinks was the first outing for the primered R&C "Dream Truck."

Upper Middle: Paradise Mesa in San Diego was an early drag strip. It was basically a flattened and paved mountaintop, a World War II Navy practice landing field. An amateur operation run by a group of twenty clubs operating as the San Diego Timing Association from 1951 to 1957, it spawned many name racers and used Otto Crocker's clocks. This is Paul Schiefer, of racing clutch fame, smoking off in his streamlined rear-engined lakes-and-drags 1927 T.

Lower Middle: Saint Vasques was a member of the Renegades of Long Beach car club, along with Larry Watson, Duane Steck, and so many other well-known names. Although Saint's chopped Titian Red 1950 Chevy convertible was highly modified: molded 1953 grille shell, 1955 DeSoto grille, Cadillac headlights, Packard taillights, Olds windshield, etc. It was featured in only one magazine that gave no credit for bodywork, paint, or upholstery.

Bottom: No photo says "backyard builder" better than this one. Plus, it epitomizes the Depression Era genesis of rodding: build it yourself, from whatever you've got, using whatever else you can get. This 1930 A roadster is only a few years old (photo is dated July 21, 1938) but it already looks well used. The owner has chopped and raked the windshield, added 1932 bumpers, possibly a high-compression head on the stock four, and one chrome wheelcover on mismatched tires. This is just the start.

All photographs in this book are from the Pat Ganahl Collection. Many of the vintage photos in this book are of lower quality. They have been included because of their importance to telling the story.

OVERSEAS DISTRIBUTION BY:

PGUK
63 Hatton Garden
London EC1N 8LE, England
Phone: 020 7061 1980 • Fax: 020 7242 3725
www.pguk.co.uk

Renniks Publications Ltd.
3/37-39 Green Street
Banksmeadow, NSW 2109, Australia
Phone: 2 9695 7055 • Fax: 2 9695 7355
www.renniks.com

Table of Contents

Introduction 6

Chapter One: Hop-Ups, Gow Jobs and Modifieds 10

Chapter Two: On the Street 36

Chapter Three: The First Car Shows 60

Chapter Four: The First Drag Strips 82

Chapter Five: The Early Customs 104

Chapter Six: Early Hot Rod Shops and Speed Parts 126

Chapter Seven: Car Shows, Angel Hair and Tiki Heads 142

Chapter Eight: 1950s Hot Rods in Color 158

Chapter Nine: 1950s Customs in Color 174

Introduction

This is the good stuff. I've been saving it for a long time. Now is the time to share it. Any of you who've been reading my material for a while know that I have always been concerned with recording, writing, and preserving the history of this thing we call hot rodding. This, of course, includes custom cars, drag racing, car shows, rod runs, and so many other aspects of fixing up, racing, personalizing, and showing off cars that have been modified or rebuilt by individuals, following certain patterns or trends, at least since the Depression days of the early 1930s. In this book I'm not going to tell the history of hot rodding, I'm going to show it.

I'm not sure when I consciously started collecting early hot rod photos. The first of this type I ever took myself were at the first Winternationals drags and car show in Pomona in 1961, when I was 13. I had a cheap, used 35-mm camera, and my dad showed me how to process the black-and-white film and make prints in our makeshift bathroom darkroom at home. I still have those negatives. I also have all the car magazines I bought back then, and even some of the custom models I built. I'm not sure how I kept them, but I've always collected this sort of stuff.

I've filled out my magazine collection with most of the earlier copies I was too young to buy when they were new, and in most cases I was able to go back to Volume I, Number 1. This was because, in large part, older friends gave me issues that they had saved and stored in boxes, knowing that they'd never read them again but that I would use them for reference. I bought other issues at swap meets or from dealers. They are the tools of my trade.

I've built my own personal hot rod photo archive in much the same way. It now numbers somewhere between 30,000 and 40,000 images. It's impossible to count; I can only estimate.

The Beginning of the Archive

It began sometime after I stumbled into my first job at *Street Rodder* magazine in late 1973. As I write this, that was exactly forty years ago. It took me a couple of years to learn the ropes, including how to take magazine-quality photographs with the proper equipment. I began doing historical articles right away, starting with a couple on *Street Rodder*'s founder/publisher Tom McMullen and his legendary flamed 1932 hiboy roadster. Having been an avid freelancer in earlier days, Tom had lots of older photos of this car and others that I could use for these stories. I loved this "archival" stuff; it whetted my appetite.

My own collecting of such photos started a bit later, and was pure serendipity. It began with "the Box." When I joined *Street Rodder* the magazine was just over a year old, and for a long time it had no designated ad sales person. When they finally hired Bill Burke for that position and introduced him to me, I admit I didn't know who he was. When I learned that he was one of the first Ad Managers of *Hot Rod* magazine, the inventor of the belly

> *"I loved this 'archival' stuff; it whetted my appetite."*

tank lakester, and so much more, I immediately proposed doing a lengthy historical article on him. He reluctantly produced a stack of amazing early photos and acted as if it were old hat (which, for him, it actually was). He quickly saw how enthusiastic I was about this early stuff that went back to the 1930s. I hadn't known that any of it existed. The readers found it equally entertaining and exciting.

So not too long after, Bill comes whistling into my small office, a big grin on his face, plunks down a cardboard box on my desk, and says, "Here, you have more interest in this old stuff than I do. Keep it and use it." I swear the dusty old box had purple paint spilled on it, and a jumble of stuff inside, topped by a large, old photo album, its covers tied together with a shoestring. The covers also had paint splotches and remnants of old stickers. The pages inside were black, with little black glue-on "corners" to hold many small photos, each with captions hand-written in black pencil below. Trying to read the captions was almost impossible because nearly all of the photos had fallen out of their holders and were scattered throughout the box.

As I dug deeper into this treasure trove, I discovered black-and-white prints from different decades, envelopes full of crinkly-edged photos of Bill's earliest hot rods on the street and dry lakes, and similar photos of lots of other cars. I also found a number of envelopes full of negatives ranging from 2 x 3 medium format to 4 x 5s. Among these were some old trophies, several early lakes timing tags, and buttons and ribbons reading "Chief Starter" and "Floor Manager First Hot Rod Show."

What I didn't realize at first was that one of the members of Bill's first club in the 1930s and 1940s, the Road Rebels, was Jack Peters, who created and published the first hot rod magazine, *Throttle*, in 1941. Peters had some decent cameras and took candid photos of club happenings as well as lakes racing at Muroc. When he shut down the magazine and went off to war, he gave all of his photos and negs to Bill. Contact proofs of these photos were originally mounted in the album, but the original negatives were scattered throughout the box, unfortunately unprotected, and kind of scratched up. However, they were still the original negs and included the *Throttle* cover shots. Having been involved in the hot rod magazine business since its inception, being a founding member of Southern California Timing Association (SCTA), and a competitor at every Bonneville with a wild variety of record-setting machines, Bill collected all sorts of photos well into the 1960s and 1970s, until he gave them to me. It was quite a hodgepodge and took me a long time to sort out, but it was an incredible foundation for building a hot rod photo archive.

More Than Just Photos

My penchant for finding "lost" rods and customs also started early on, beginning with McMullen's roadster and Tommy Ivo's T. In 1976, when a lot of hot rod folks, including Ed "Big Daddy" Roth, had simply disappeared, I happened on most of Roth's wild fiberglass cars in a museum called Cars of the Stars, just blocks from the *Street Rodder* offices. Through its owner, Jimmie Brucker, I subsequently found Roth working as a soft-spoken, clean-shaven, Mormon sign-painter at nearby Knott's Berry Farm. He was more than happy to let me do a "rediscovery" article on him in the magazine, and produced plenty of old photos from his files for me to use.

As it turned out, Roth was a pretty good photographer; he shot a few magazine features himself.

This led to a life-long friendship with Ed, which eventually led to complete books on him as well as another Brucker "favorite," Von Dutch. Brucker was the world's greatest collector of everything, so these projects unearthed lots of rare vintage photographs that the people involved not only let me use, but also said I could copy with my own camera to add to my photo archive. I won't forget one long evening when I drove up to Sacramento to Roth's older brother's house, set up lights and a tripod, and photographed pictures of young Ed from a family album on a coffee table the night before his brother left for a two-year mission to Mongolia.

A combination of hot rod archeology and serendipity led to numerous images in my collection. For example, I met Dick Bertolucci as a member of Inliners International, racing six-cylinders at the first nostalgia drags at Fremont in the 1980s. When I found out he was a custom builder from the early days in Sacramento, my first question was, "Did you know Harry Westergard?" Dick's deadpan answer was, "Yes, he worked for me." Well, this quickly led to a good-sized article on the "Capitol Clan," including Westergard, Bertolucci, the young Barris brothers, and other founding members of the Thunderbolts car club. Many of these guys had great, never-before-seen photos of Westergard, various cars he built, some of Bertolucci's beautiful work, and more. One member, Norm Milne, who drove a very nice V-windshield 1931 roadster, had a good camera and actually sent me his original 2 x 3 negatives to keep.

Generosity was a huge ingredient in building my photo collection. Much of my photo collecting has been done directly out of people's albums. I copied their images with my camera wherever I could find a convenient spot with open, even lighting. Dick Bertolucci had three or four such albums, covering everything from his first chicken-shack custom shop, to early GMC drag racing, to Bonneville. So I found a good spot in his driveway in Sacramento, laid the albums out, and copied the mostly black-and-white photos with my own camera and film, so I could keep the negatives in my files. You'll see a few of those photos here.

This brings up two points. The first is that, early on, whenever I found an early rodder or customizer (or a bystander or photographer) who had a good collection of decent early photos, I would ask if I could borrow the photos and copy them for my collection, for possible use in future articles or books. If they'd let me, I'd take them home and photograph each print on a makeshift copy stand. If not, I'd ask if I could photograph them right there, which I often did.

The second point has two parts. In the case of Dick Bertolucci's albums, they included some cool photos he took at George and Sam Barris' early shop, when he and his new bride Bev drove down to Los Angeles on their honeymoon in 1948. In one shot George is wearing a sailor hat and grinning, along with several buddies, behind a flamed track roadster with "Barris's Custom" painted on the wall above the shop door. It's a great early photo, and I've used it in articles a few times. I don't think Dick has let anyone else copy it. Yet I have seen this photo reproduced a number of times, even in surprising places. The point is that in our digital age, with Photoshop and similar capabilities, once a photo is printed (or, worse, copied to the internet), it can show up almost anywhere. The other side of that coin, especially early on, was that people who gladly let me copy their old photos, also gladly let almost anyone else copy them, which was fine. In my case, this applies particularly to several early Orange County/Santa Ana images that came from sign-painter Eldon "Snappy" Snapp, Stan Betz, Dick Kraft, Marvin Webb, and so on.

"Every Picture Tells a Story"

So, given that I had to winnow some 30,000 to 40,000 images down to about 350 of the best to show here, what were the criteria? It wasn't easy. First of all, I've limited this book to the 1930s, 1940s, and 1950s (with perhaps a little spillage into the early 1960s). This was unquestionably the time of the birth and growth: the golden era of

> "Most of the photos were taken in black-and-white, and nearly all the photographers were amateurs, generally using cheap cameras."

hot rodding and customizing. Hoping that you like this one and buy a whole lot of 'em presumes a second volume. That one would cover the 1960s, 1970s, and 1980s encompassing the Fuel Era in drag racing, the birth of street rodding, the rebirth of Kustom Kars, nostalgia drag racing, national rod runs, and more. I have plenty more good stuff in my photo files covering those historic eras.

However, since I'm starting at the beginning, before World War II and even in the depths of the Depression, you have to understand that most of the photos were taken in black-and-white, and nearly all the photographers were amateurs, generally using cheap cameras. Furthermore, even many of the "professional" negatives I have (such as those from the bottom of Bill Burke's box) have been poorly kept, abused, and scratched. Even the newest of these photos are now more than fifty years old.

Consequently, I have selected these specific photos for a variety of reasons. This is a book about hot rods and custom cars, so the first priority had to be that the cars were either historically significant or just plan cool in one way or another. On the other hand, this is not a history book, it's a photo gallery, so I don't take pains to identify each car or person in each photo. I will when I can, but other details in the photo are more important.

There are pictures in my files that you've seen plenty of times, so another priority was to select fresh images you haven't seen. Because I had so many to choose from, I tried to select the sharper, better exposed, less scratchy photos as often as possible. However, other qualities of the photo were actually more important to me, such as the subject matter, camera angle, composition, lighting, and so on. If there's action in a photo, it's dynamic. A certain mood or ambiance in the image should be apparent.

I also tried to select photos with people in them as often as possible. Who were the first hot rodders? What did they look like? I cover three decades here, and styles changed. In addition to the distinctive styles of the cars, I also wanted to show clothing, hairstyles, even attitudes of the people interacting with the cars.

The two photos I have presented in this introduction demonstrate this range. The black-and-white shot of Earl Evans' flamed belly tank being pushed off at Bonneville has almost Ansel Adams–like tonal qualities: the white salt, dark mountains in the distance, darkening cloud-filled sky overhead, and the perspective of the cones and lines leading to a point in the distance, where the car will run. The sleek, small bullet shape of the open-wheel race car dwarfed by the bulky pickup adds further dimension. But the starters, one holding the flag, but more so the other on tiptoe pointing in different directions, add a dynamic quality to this otherwise still photo, that you'd never see in an Ansel Adams landscape. Cars, especially hot rods and race cars, can be tremendously dynamic, but the photographer has to catch the right second to capture and convey it.

The other photograph, from the same era, presents a completely different scene. The camera's low angle does not show off the sleek lines or colors of Jay Johnston's custom Ford to best advantage. It does enhance the composition of the domed roof on the left, white square lattice on the right, with a flagstone wall in between (including the ubiquitous palm), for a setting that is perfectly mid-century modern, as is the customized Ford. Add Jay's perky girlfriend in her black checked slacks, slightly windblown bouffant hair, bright red lipstick in a come-on smile and gaze directed right at the photographer, as well as a leaned-back stance that not only towers over the chopped roofline, but says, "Yeah, the car looks good, but so do I," and you have a great, classic photo.

This is not just a picture of a cool car; it's a great photo that includes a cool car. You'll see several variations on this theme throughout the book. If a few of the images look familiar to you, I've included them primarily because they are great, classic hot rod or custom car photos. I figured you wouldn't mind seeing them again, and they're reproduced here from the original negatives or color transparency film.

Beyond that, I repeat that this is primarily a photo gallery, so text is at a minimum; as much room as possible is left for photos. As Rod Stewart sang so famously, "Every picture tells a story." These do. I think you'll enjoy it.

CHAPTER ONE

Hop-Ups, Gow Jobs and Modifieds

Plenty of dissention exists about when hot rodding actually started, or what constituted the first hot rods. Going by the oft-cited definition that a hot rod is a production vehicle modified by the owner for improved performance and/or beauty, I could easily argue that Henry Ford was the first hot rodder because he made the first production-line car, the Model T, and then he modified several of them to set numerous speed records.

Auto racing became a craze across the United States during the 1910s and 1920s, with stripped-down fenderless cars racing on city-street circuits, county fair horse tracks, dirt ovals, board tracks, and even flat, hard beaches. During this time dozens of small companies made cylinder heads, intake manifolds, carburetors, and other components to "hop-.up" cars, primarily Model Ts, for such racing. Others produced cut-down "speedster" bodies. Even Ford Motor Company's own *Ford Times* magazine gave explicit directions for modifying Model T engines, chassis, and bodies for such racing. Several such modified Ts competed successfully in early Indy 500s; one finished fifth.

Nevertheless, I contend that these weren't the first hot rods. They provided some of the source material, and likewise some of the inspiration, for what would become hot rods. It is my long-held belief that those cars that were tagged with the name "hot rod" after World War II actually were a result of and developed because of the Great Depression that followed the stock market crash of 1929.

Jobs evaporated, prices tumbled, and certainly the high-cost auto-racing craze ceased almost immediately. Young guys, just reaching driving age, who had seen this racing frenzy (possibly through the streets or at the fairgrounds of their hometown), wanted cars to drive. Some wanted flashy, fast cars like the Mercers and Stutzes they had seen in the 1920s. Others wanted to build cars to race. Nobody had money to buy fancy cars, and most of the racetracks had closed.

Nobody seems to know exactly when the first organized top-speed races were held at Muroc dry lake in the high desert northeast of Los Angeles. We know some timed record runs were staged there in the early 1920s. But whether regular, organized timed meets began there in the late 1920s or early 1930s is not as important as the fact that young guys in the Los Angeles area knew that these wide, hard, flat dry lakes were up there. These

> "It was a do-it-yourself enterprise, and the racing was strictly amateur: for fun and honor, not money."

young guys were the ones who had scrounged cast-off Model T, Chevrolet, or other cheap roadster bodies, frames, and engines from junkyards. They were rebuilding them and hopping them up in high school shop classes. They knew that you could run cars across the dry lakes as fast as possible without fear of police or other intervention.

During this time George Wight turned his junkyard on Gage Avenue in Bell, California, into Bell Auto Parts, and specialized in selling used "speed equipment" stripped off defunct race cars (as well as cheap, complete "used" race cars). Lee Chapel was doing similar business at his "speed shop" on San Fernando Road south of Glendale. In fact, some folks cite Wight as the first to start organized timed speed trails at Muroc, as the Bell Timing Association in spring 1931.

Who and when is not as important as the fact that this was a new kind of racing participated in by enthusiastic, like-minded young guys who had built their own fast and cheap roadsters out of cast-off and used parts. These cars were light and quick, and nearly all doubled as street transportation, since few could afford a second, dedicated race car. It was natural that they would engage in impromptu acceleration contests, side-by-side on city streets. These contests were, of course, both illegal and dangerous; the dry lakes were the perfect place. At some early point these straight-line "dig outs" became known as "drag" racing.

There are some other terms that have become connected with hot rods. I've stated that "hot rod" wasn't used until sometime during the mid 1940s. I have no idea who coined it or how it developed, although most agree it was a shortening of "hot roadster," in typical slang fashion. It might have also grown from "hop-up," which

From Bill Burke's scrapbook, this photo is simply titled "Muroc 1939 Finish Line." The Model A roadster flying down the flagged course at more than 100 mph gives a hint of how broad, flat, and big Muroc was. Numerous dry lakes dot the high desert north and east of Los Angeles. Organized speed trials were held at Muroc, Rosamond, Harper, and El Mirage, depending on weather and surface conditions, but of these Muroc was by far the largest. Closed to racers in November 1941, it is now Edwards Air Force Base, where the space shuttles landed. El Mirage, where the Southern California Timing Association (SCTA) meets have been held since the end of World War II, is about one-tenth the size.

---

was one of the names these young guys used during the 1930s for their stripped-down cars with built-up engines. In an interview with Ed Iskenderian, describing the roadster he built in 1938, he says, "Hop-ups, soup ups, gow jobs; yeah, that's what we called them. We didn't have the name hot rod yet."

Who knows how youth-oriented slang develops but this new endeavor (you could call it a trend, fad, or craze) soon included its own esoteric jargon. "Hot" has long been a term meaning "good," but it also denotes power. "Hotted up" could describe a girl with flashy clothes and makeup, just as well as an engine (or car) with added carbs, pipes, and other speed parts. "Hop" and "weed"

Chapter One: Hop-Ups, Gow Jobs and Modifieds

were drug terms from the jazz age; "hopped up" could describe not only a person but also a race horse injected with drugs to make it run faster.

"Souped up" could mean the same thing, or it could have derived from "supe" as in "super."

"Gow," on the other hand (rhymes with "now"), obviously comes from "go." But when I asked Wally Parks what it meant, he said, "It comes from the sound a hot roadster makes when it takes off." Well, these souped-up hop-ups had a lot of gow.

In this chapter I refer to modifieds, lakesters, and streamliners. These are class designations used when lakes racing became organized. A modified is a narrow, single-seat roadster made from a 1920s racer or more often by cutting and narrowing a Model T or similar roadster body, often with a more streamlined nose or grille for less wind resistance. Any such car with a tear-drop or similar-shaped tail behind the driver's seat was classed as a streamliner. After the war, streamliners became envelope-bodied cars with enclosed wheels, while open-wheel versions (such as belly tanks) became lakesters.

However, my purpose here is not to *tell* you the story of the birth of hot rodding, but to *show* you. Let me sum up by saying that this new car culture was born largely in, and because of, the Depression. Young guys who could build light, fast, loud roadsters from cheap parts with their own mechanical skill and ingenuity (often helping each other) developed this new form of racing. They started a new kind of straight-line acceleration racing that, given the lack of other racing venues, could be indulged in at the drop of a hat on any city street, but gravitated to the safer, broad, flat dry lakes.

One last important distinction is that they banded together in clubs with names like Knight Riders, Vultures, Road Runners, and Low Flyers. These were not gangs. They were more like counter-culture fraternities with a common interest. It was a do-it-yourself enterprise, and the racing was strictly amateur: for fun and honor, not money. In fact, it still is. Here's how it looked when it started.

> "From the beginning, the majority of lakes racers were street roadsters stripped of their fenders, lights, windshields, etc."

What did the first "hot rods" look like? You probably didn't expect something like this. It uses a Model A frame and four-cylinder with some sort of overhead conversion (given the carburetor placement). The narrow handmade body makes it a Modified, which was the most aerodynamic, and therefore fastest, class in the early 1930s. The front wire wheels came from an earlier race car; they are akin to mag wheels today. Yes, it had shiny paint and even upholstery.

Perhaps this Modified is closer to what you had in mind because it uses a narrowed Model T body. The three-spring frame, wire wheels (check out the handmade knockoffs), and Rajo-head T engine all likely came from 1920s race cars. The grille, like most of the car, is hand-fabbed. Early roadster clubs were multi-cultural; the Mercuries were mostly Afro-American. This might be "Rajo Jack's" car.

Hot Rod Gallery 13

From the beginning, the majority of lakes racers were street roadsters stripped of their fenders, lights, windshields, etc. The stripping often happened at the lake, upon arrival. What's notable about this late 1930s photo is the Riley-headed four-cylinder (instead of a V-8) in the whitewalled 1932, and the dressy clothes the owners are wearing, not to mention some pricey cars in the background. The roadster boys were mostly blue-collar, but certainly not exclusively.

These young guys in T-shirts with their fenderless 1929 A come close to the stereotype of early hot rodders, right? The goofy hat and water bag on the door are good touches. It's not shiny, and there's no chrome anywhere, but the car is painted; note the filled cowl and Deuce shell. The artillery wheels are unusual, and it's interesting that the windshield and bullet headlights are in place (for now). The strangest part is what appears to be some sort of flathead-six topped with an early McCulloch supercharger. The point is, there were no stereotypes, especially in the early days. Each owner-built car was unique.

I got this photo from Duke Hallock years ago. He was the maker of the namesake V-windshields for Model As and owner of the car (with windshield removed) in front proudly wearing No. 1. He wrote at the bottom, "The other two windshields . . . Muroc races, May 16, 1937 . . . 118.42 mph."

> "You can almost see and hear the action in this photo."

You can almost see and hear the action in this photo. Arnold Birner was the best-known member of the Bungholers club, and Burke penciled in his scrapbook, "4-Port Riley, 118.48, Turtle deck flew open." Note that it wears a license plate for regular street use.

It's often stated that Norm Grabowski invented the T-Bucket. He gave it his own look, yes, but the style goes back to rodding's beginnings, as exemplified by numerous variations on the theme throughout this book. With its abbreviated body, V-8 engine with "lakes" pipes, and an excellent big-and-little tire combo, Howard McKesson's Modified would look great today.

No. 333's stock-width body puts it in the roadster class, where it ran 103.80; not shabby for a flathead Model A four in the late 1930s. The two-spring front frame, 1929 A grille, and short wheelbase make it look kind of kooky, huh? I love it.

Hot Rod Gallery   15

I've shown this action shot before, but it's such a great photo that it's worth repeating. Besides, it's straight from the first issue of *Throttle* magazine (January 1941). That's Tony Capanna (later of Wilcap Company) piloting Jim Harrell's (as in Harrell V-8 heads, etc.) highly modified T to a Western Timing Association two-way record of 121.46 mph. Harrell's T was powered by a Hudson straight-8 engine. The date was July 14, 1940, and the look on Tony's face as he unstraps his cloth "helmet" is priceless.

"This is another great example of one more variation on the T-Bucket (known in those days as a Modified) theme."

Several of these early photos came from the collection of multi-talented long-time hot rodder and 9-inch rear-end king, Frank Currie. This is another great example of one more variation on the T-Bucket (known in those days as a Modified) theme. This one incorporates a full hood for streamlining, a Ford V-8, and a raked 1934 grille. I really like the driver's jaunty stance.

This is one of the most famous, enduring, fabulous, successful, yet enigmatic hot rods of all time. You know it today, in its restored form, as Art Chrisman's No. 25 dragster. I found this photo of it, leaving the starting line at Muroc sometime in the 1930s, in Bill Burke's scrapbook with no caption or identification. The earliest photos I've seen of it are in a biography of Roy Richter (of Bell and Cragar) by Art Bagnall. It's shown outside as well as in the showroom of Bell Auto Parts, and the captions say it ran a Rajo head at the dry lakes and circle tracks, but gives no name. Even then it had the Eddie Miller–style nose and fully chromed suspension, including rear axle. The most information I've found on its early history is in a four-paragraph box in Dean Batchelor's seminal *American Hot Rod*, calling it a "Harry Lewis–built Modified."

Frank Currie had this photo of the car at Muroc, with a Cragar four (made by Bell) with four carbs; the wire-wheel knock-offs are marked "BELL." Batchelor's book says Jack Harvey ran it this way in 1938 and 1939, and then sold it to Ernie McAfee, who installed a Ford V-8 in late 1939. All this time it was white. Then Jack Lehman got it and reportedly painted it red in 1942. Finally, Doug Caruthers acquired it, painted it black, and ran it after the war until LeRoy Neumayer and Chrisman got it and turned it into a dragster. You'll see more of it throughout the book. Somebody needs to tell the whole history of this car.

Hot Rod Gallery   17

Here are a couple never-before-seen photos of another historic car. In the Modified version, Bill Burke misidentified it first as being Karl Orr's (whose similar white car won the SCTA championship in 1942), then correctly (?) as belonging to Jack Harvey. In the shot with the streamlined tail added, taken by Frank Currie sometime after 1938, he noted that it was Bill Warth's, and was running a Winfield flathead four. It became Stu Hilborn's in 1942.

Jack Peters probably took this great low-angle picture of Bill Burke in his own, first, race-only lakes Modified. He built it in 1937 using a Chrysler grille, narrowed 1927 T body, Chevy frame rails, Franklin front axle and dual springs, Model A rear, and a Winfield Red Head Model B engine with Stromberg carbs on a Cragar intake. It set a 110-mph class record at Muroc, and began a life-long endeavor for Bill.

Chapter One *Hop-Ups, Gow Jobs and Modifieds*

Everybody agreed it was ugly. Even builder Ernie McAfee who painted the "whiskers" on the front, but the No. 1 attests it was fast. This was the first streamliner with a completely handmade body, and it won the SCTA points championship in its first year of existence (1938), running 132 mph with a Winfield flathead Model B four-cylinder. This new class applied to Modifieds with any type of streamlined tail behind the seat. Check out the Chevy C-cab Good Humors ice cream truck in the background.

Young Bob Rufi, in a stocking cap under the plastic bubble, did a much finer job crafting the teardrop-shaped body for his small streamliner, refining the concept with wheel covers and axle fairings. Running a small Chevy four-cylinder with an Olds three-port head, he stunned everyone with a 140-mph two-way average speed in 1940, a record that stood for several years. Note the guy to the right with a twin-lens Rollei around his neck, one of the few at the lakes with a good camera.

Not only is this a fantastic action shot, showing "Bill Weber in his supercharged Modified leading Eddie Meyer II at a Western Timing meet," but it was also the cover photo of the March 1941 issue of *Throttle* magazine: this is the actual 5 x 7 print that was used. It was taped in Burke's album (with crop marks on it), under one of Bill's timing tags (Car No. 16, C/ST, 136.15 mph) from 1947. Weber ran "120 flat," and yes, they ran side-by-side "drag" races at the lakes early on.

Hot Rod Gallery   19

One of Rufi's buddies, Ralph Schenk, built a similar Chevy-powered streamliner using aircraft-building techniques in 1938. I love the action shot of a Road Runners club member grabbing a photo as it crosses the finish line on a return run.

This close-up shows Schenk trying to coax more speed from the small four. I think the similarity to Barney Oldfield's *Golden Submarine* is coincidental. Schenk left his in bare aluminum; the metalwork is phenomenal.

Here it's obviously postwar at El Mirage, probably close to 1950. The unusual though nicely crafted car has a dropped Ford axle, 1937 truck grille, and a 1929 cowl with no visible body behind it. Given the placement of carbs and pipes, I'd guess the engine is a big Cadillac V-16.

Chapter One *Hop-Ups, Gow Jobs and Modifieds*

"It has shiny paint and yet all four tires are bald. This is a great image of a 1930s rodder and his ride."

At first I thought this was Bill Burke, but it's one of his young, blond-haired buddies. The plate says 1939. The big headlights and chromed 1932 grille were unusual for the time. The running boards and mechanical brakes are still in place. I have no idea what engine is in it, although the hood is off to show it. It has shiny paint and yet all four tires are bald. This is a great image of a 1930s rodder and his ride.

As you can imagine, there were plenty of photos in Bill Burke's box of his various belly tanks, including many construction shots of this one, the first. This might even be a cold day in late 1946, after Howard Wilson bought it and cut off the tail to make it a Modified (running 140.40 best). I like the way the two guys are patting its sides, while it waits to make a run, as if wishing it good luck.

Hot Rod Gallery 21

Burke got the brilliant idea to make aerodynamic race cars out of World War II aluminum teardrop auxiliary aircraft fuel tanks, available as surplus right after the war. However, he quickly realized that his first front-engine design was too small, so he switched to this larger P-38 tank with the engine in the rear. Painted his signature color "Burple" (metallic purple), this "Sweet 16" set the 1947 SCTA C Streamliner record at 139.21 mph (two-way average). It was often driven by Wally Parks, as seen here in an excellent angle taken from the timing stand by Jack Mickelson.

Although it's pretty dusty, this is how the "No. 25" car looked when Doug Caruthers owned it in the late 1940s. He must have attached some sort of tail to it, because it set the SCTA B Streamliner record at 136.39 in 1947. I have several photos of it (including Wally Parks driving), but I like this one because of the interesting crowd gathered to watch it take off.

> "If you want to know what hot rodders looked like back then, this is a good portrait: a little bit of everything."

This is no action photo, but there's still a whole lot going on in this "pits" picture from the 1940s at El Mirage. Most of the race cars are 1929 roadsters with 1939 taillights, but there's one Carson-topped custom in the background (at left). Given the attire, including bell bottoms, a P-coat, and various Navy caps, I'd guess it was shortly after the war, and apparently a warm day after a typically cold, dry lakes morning. I'm a bit surprised there are no ladies present, because they were part of the scene. But if you want to know what hot rodders looked like back then, this is a good portrait: a little bit of everything.

Jack Mickelson had one of the nicer 1932 Ford roadsters in the late 1940s, and he must have had a good camera because he sent me a bunch of excellent photos to copy for my collection when I was researching his fellow Vultures club member Joe Nitti's *Deep Purple* Deuce hiboy. This one shows young Mark Smith of the Glendale Sidewinders adjusting his goggles in his stripped-down A-V-8 street roadster before a run of over 120 mph in 1947. After World War II, hot rodding became essentially a teen craze in SoCal, and I think this photo typifies it perfectly.

Hot Rod Gallery 23

You think there are too many look-alike 1932 hiboys today? Nothing's new. Note that all of these cars have windshield stanchions, indicating removal of street equipment for racing. The car in front is unusual, especially in California, because it's channeled. This is another photo that typifies rodders and their roadsters in the later 1940s.

After acquiring the Warth car in 1942, Stuart Hilborn rebuilt it with the help of neighbor Eddie Miller, Jr. After installing an early flathead V-8 and painting it a beautiful black, he made one run before Muroc was closed by the army. Accounts vary, but Stuart told me the spokes broke in his left rear wheel, causing the car to flip and roll at speed at El Mirage in August 1947. This Burke photo appears to confirm his story. It makes you wonder how Hilborn survived this wreck with only a broken back; it had no roll bar and no room to duck inside.

Chapter One *Hop-Ups, Gow Jobs and Modifieds*

Nearly as amazing as Hilborn surviving the wreck is how Eddie Miller reshaped the mangled body during Hilborn's three-week hospital stay. Then it was featured on the cover of the April 1948 issue of *Hot Rod Magazine (HRM)*, and on July 17, 1948, it broke the 150-mph barrier, clocking 150.50 one-way on a 146-mph record. Even more amazing is that he used a 1934 21-stud engine with stock (filled) heads and a hand-ground cam, on straight alcohol. The trick was Hilborn's revolutionary, handmade, constant-flow fuel injection system, for which he became deservedly famous. The photo above, with Howie Wilson driving, was taken just before the historic run. I've seen it printed elsewhere, but this is from the original negative, which was in the bottom of Bill Burke's box.

> "Nearly as amazing as Hilborn surviving the wreck is how Eddie Miller reshaped the mangled body during Hilborn's three-week hospital stay."

Hot Rod Gallery 25

Here's another fantastic action photo. Bill Burke built more than a dozen belly tanks for other racers; he painted this one Burple for the Stanford Brothers and Phy. It's proudly wearing the big No. 1 at El Mirage in 1951 because it was the SCTA points champion for 1950; it ran a 246-inch Merc in the B Lakester class.

I have way too many photos of crashed cars, both at the lakes and at the drags, but I won't dwell on them. I include this one to show the diverse crowd of onlookers. Note that the flipped A-V-8 has taillights, a 1947 license plate, and an unidentifiable club plaque. Rocker Brian Setzer used this photo on the cover of one of his albums.

26 Chapter One *Hop-Ups, Gow Jobs and Modifieds*

Jack Calori is deservedly renowned for his archetypal, LaSalle-grille custom 1936 Ford coupe from the November 1949 *HRM* cover, but he actually built that car to tow this quick (128 mph), good-looking, black-lacquer roadster with a Clay Smith flathead. Long Beach metal-man Herb Reneau molded the doors shut, formed the hood with blisters for the upswept pipes, and faired-in the front and rear license plates. What's intriguing about this 1946 photo, in addition to the high angle on this great roadster, is the custom coupe behind it with the molded vertical grille and low-set headlights that predates Calori's. Moreover, it's not a 1936 Ford; is it a Willys or possibly a Lincoln Zephyr?

Randy Shinn's very low and very fast (over 130 mph) 1927 T had a streamlined nose and probably wore taillights and license plate for flat towing to the lakes. The camera angle and the flying dirt make this a great photo, but I show it primarily to illustrate the bad, or loose, lake surface. This could cause cars to get sideways, dig in, and then flip. The loose surface wasn't caused by over-use (as many argued); it was caused by weather. One good, hard rain, followed by a day of hot sun would level this surface perfectly smooth and bake the alkali-adobe brick-hard once again.

Hot Rod Gallery   27

Not only are these two black 1929 roadsters good-looking and nearly identical (one had a four, the other a V-8), but I think this photo depicts the booming postwar period of hot rodding: healthy young kids with well-built, well-dressed roadsters. It wasn't the Depression anymore. Jack Clifford (on the left) had a good job as a pattern maker and made the quick-change rear ends for these rods. Tom Morris (on the right) worked in a chrome shop, so his Sharp-equipped V-8 was *very* well dressed. He later painted it red with cream wheels and kept it exactly like this all his life; his widow still has it.

The amazing, perpetually enthusiastic Dick Kraft gave me dozens of photos to copy over the years; this is one of my favorites. It's his "blue" roadster, stripped for racing at El Mirage in the late 1940s, largely built by Marvin Webb with an Ingels nose. It's an excellent car, and I love the wild action of the three guys pushing him off, frozen at that second by the camera.

Chapter One Hop-Ups, Gow Jobs and Modifieds

I visited "Big George" Bentley at his old house in East Los Angeles when I was searching for photos or clues about the Joe Nitti roadster. The Sadd-Teague-Bentley roadster was sitting in the small wooden garage in back, and I waited there as he brought out a cigar box filled with old photos of Vultures club members, lakes, Santa Ana drags, and more. This one is fuzzy; maybe "hazy" is a better word because it has that atmosphere, as George rests in his roadster while someone else runs for ice cream in the dusty little town of Adelanto on the way home from a hot, dry day of racing at El Mirage.

Here's another gem from Bentley's cigar box. How many hot rodders does it take to quickly change a tire on a roadster at El Mirage? Just about this many, when a jack's not handy. Note that the girls are neither helping, nor interested.

Hot Rod Gallery   29

"How many hot rodders does it take to quickly change a tire on a roadster at El Mirage?"

Jim Woods was known for making Ford flathead sixes go fast, and this is his wickedly chopped Bantam coupe, perhaps the first of this breed in racing (it was later owned by Bill Burke, then by Mickey Thompson, who ran it with two different engines: a flathead and a Chrysler Hemi). What makes this a great photo is the placement and the diversity of the cars at the starting line, plus the guy in the club jacket with the little cigar leaning over to give Jim some last words of advice, almost like a trainer in a boxer's corner before the last round. The No. 39 Deuce roadster is Dean Batchelor's.

"What makes this a great photo is the placement and the diversity of the cars at the starting line."

Chapter One *Hop-Ups, Gow Jobs and Modifieds*

One source identifies the guy in the helmet as Don Corwin. I'm not sure why he's driving, but that's a young Fran Hernandez holding the door of his own beautiful black 1932 coupe at an early Russetta timing meet at El Mirage. Running at more than 122 mph, it graced the April 1949 *HRM* cover, and it won the infamous "blower versus nitro" grudge race against Tom Cobbs at the Goleta drags that year. Working at Offenhauser, then Edelbrock, Fran parlayed his hot rod experience into a life-long career heading Ford's various performance divisions, including eminent successes at Le Mans and Indy.

Since Don Montgomery has shown so many photos of other early hot rodders and their cars in his many books over the last couple of decades, I thought it only fitting to show this image I found in my files. That's a very young Don leaning over the six-carb Jimmy six in his coffin-nose Cord sedan. Previously powered by a Buick straight-8, it was the second of several serious race cars he campaigned at the lakes and early drags. That's his fellow Glendale Coupe and Roadster Club (GCRC) club member Acmo McLaughlin's similarly powered Graham Hollywood behind him in this April 1953 photo.

Hot Rod Gallery 31

Choppers are hot rod motorcycles. This hardtail Harley with ape-hanger handlebars and a fully chromed springer front end was a nice one for 1953; it was attending a Russetta meet at El Mirage just to spectate. Don't overlook some cool machinery in the background.

It's hard to imagine how this 1939 or 1940 Ford coupe got so munched at an early Russetta lakes meet. It obviously flipped and rolled, back end first. The good news is that the aircraft bucket seat and steering wheel both remain intact, possibly because of a hidden roll bar in there, meaning the driver likely survived.

Chapter One *Hop-Ups, Gow Jobs and Modifieds*

I wish the photo quality were a little better; still, this is a classic image of enthusiastic, undaunted young rodders tearing into their chopped-top 1934 five-window coupe at an early 1950s lakes meet. The trans is out and the engine is partially disassembled; it appears they have multiple problems. And, since there's a hood on the ground, and the car has lights and a license on the front, I'd guess they drove up for the meet, and trailering home isn't an option.

> "You can't experience it unless you're there, but this photo gives a hint."

Because I'm going more-or-less in chronological order, the Bonneville photos come last, because the first hot rod meet there wasn't until 1949. I can't tell you exactly what these guys are doing, but that's the famous "long black line" that the race cars followed, as far and as fast as possible, toward the "floating mountain" looming just over the all-white horizon. You can't experience it unless you're there, but this photo gives a hint.

In this classic photo, suntanned head starter Bill Burke seems to be telling equally shirtless Don Waite which way to go at the 1950 Bonneville meet. Don's beautiful, heavily louvered, rear-engined 1927 T set the C Modified Roadster record that year at 162.70 mph. That was an amazing time for a flathead-powered car.

I originally thought this was Bill Likes' near-identical Deuce that took the B class at 1950 Bonneville, but the October 1950 *HRM* identifies it as the Hernandez & Meeks entry, which set the C Roadster record at 147.295. Obviously an Edelbrock "team" car, it was likely thrown together for this meet, demonstrating the simple and enduring 1932 hiboy style. I assume that's Fran Hernandez driving, with long-time Edelbrock engine builder Bobby Meeks in the pith helmet talking to starter Burke. The Stanford & Phy lakester, behind them to the right, hit 140 mph with a little Ford V-8-60 that year.

Chapter One *Hop-Ups, Gow Jobs and Modifieds*

A constant at Bonneville is the frantic rebuilding of cars and engines each night, often in motel rooms or in the parking lots outside. These workers somehow secured an indoor space, complete with a chain hoist, which the guys on the left are using to reinstall a full-house flathead into a belly tank from San Jose. The salt-sprayed 1932 roadster on the right is obviously from Burbank, but the best part is the girl at the far right handing the guy under it a big wrench.

> "A constant at Bonneville is the frantic rebuilding of cars and engines each night, often in motel rooms or in the parking lots outside."

The white, reflective Bonneville salt made for many dramatic photos, especially in black-and-white. This one is enhanced by driver Bob Ward looking back and squinting at the photographer. Also striking is the bold flame paint job, very likely applied by Earl Evans' good friend and sometime racing partner, Gil Ayala. George Bentley was also a regular driver. Running Evans heads and manifold, it hit 175 mph in 1950, and 188 the next year.

Hot Rod Gallery 35

Here's another negative I found loose in Bill Burke's box with no identification. It's sometime in the early 1950s. It's a good year at Bonneville, weather-wise, because the rock-hard salt has been blackened by dozens of cars making hundreds of runs. This apparently show-quality 1927 T street roadster has come all the way from Indiana to try its best running the black line.

"The rock-hard salt has been blackened by dozens of cars making hundreds of runs."

I copied this photo out of Dick Bertolucci's scrapbook. Although neither is mentioned in any coverage I could find of Bonneville, that's the well-known Cortopassi & Butler *Glass Slipper* on the right, running a flathead (note the pipes), and Dick's similarly 'glass-bodied *Dolphin* on the left, running a GMC six. This must be 1955 because the *Slipper* was featured in the January 1956 *HRM*, with photos taken on the salt, stating it ran 181 mph there "last year." Both cars were built as dragsters, and this is the only time they ran B-ville, as far as I know. The best part is that both still exist.

CHAPTER TWO

On the Street

Although plenty of cars were built specifically for racing at the dry lakes, most of the cars competing there had license plates. Even if their lights and windshields were easily unbolted for a day of racing, the majority of the cars there in the early days were not only driven up to the lakes to make all-out high-speed runs, but they served as daily transportation during the week, too.

You will probably also notice (especially if you live elsewhere) that most of these have California license plates. That's not provincialism on my part. The fact is that the hobby/sport/enterprise/culture that came to be called hot rodding did start in Southern California (SoCal) in the 1930s and 1940s. There are specific geographical reasons for this, which are probably obvious.

First and foremost is the climate, which allowed kids to drive stripped-down roadsters without tops daily, all year long. There's no snow on the ground and there's hardly ever any rain in the sky. Driving these roadsters was almost like riding a healthy motorcycle: nearly as quick and agile, yet a bit more practical, and certainly more roomy and comfortable if your girlfriend or buddies wanted to ride along.

However, there's more to it than that. First, this warm, dry weather meant that older cars didn't rust. The Los Angeles area was surrounded by miles of empty desert; this was a convenient place to dump an old car that had become worthless.

Second, because of the weather, more roadsters and other open-body cars were sold here than anywhere else. Many of these old, rust-free cars sitting in the deserts (for free) or in the junk yards (for very cheap) were roadsters, and there were plenty of them.

Third, although mountains border it on two sides, the whole Los Angeles/Orange County area is a desert. It's also a broad, flat flood plain that barely slopes to the ocean. Los Angeles was built horizontally, over widespread spaces. It was also a relatively young city, growing during the new auto age. People had cars and towns spread around SoCal, but they needed decent roads to get there. Most of SoCal ended up being criss-crossed by long, straight, mostly well-paved, fairly wide streets, many of which ran through bean fields and truck farms between towns. There were plenty of these straight, paved stretches of road that simply begged for side-by-side "drag" racing.

Further abetting this impromptu (or sometimes staged) activity was the fact that there was way too large a geographical area for the police to cover, plus the reality that police cars were much slower and more cumbersome than the hopped-up roadsters, and police radios weren't much better. In addition to racing, another common teenage game at the time was called "ditch the cops." It wasn't difficult to do.

"Here's a good look at the first hop-ups on the streets where they ran, with the people who built and enjoyed them."

Finally, these same geographical conditions attracted a budding aircraft industry to Southern California to build and test airplanes. Many of the young, mechanically adept "rodders" were able to get jobs in this industry and also in the smaller, support businesses. They learned many skills including machining, welding, and metal casting, but more importantly, they had access to aircraft components, especially in surplus stores.

Hot Rod Gallery

This was the genesis of hot rodding in Southern California, beginning in the Depression and evolving with the build-up to World War II. You've probably read about the second phase, when the war started and large bases, airfields, and shipyards were built in this area to train hundreds of thousands of fresh recruits from all over the country. Of course most of the over-18 roadster boys joined the war effort, leaving their hop-ups at home, often in the hands of younger brothers just old enough to have licenses. All the new recruits training in SoCal saw these loud, fast, stripped-down roadsters scooting around. They'd never seen anything like them, because these cars weren't anywhere else, and there were no magazines (or other media) showing them. They sure did look like fun.

Likewise, roadster boys shipped to other states or overseas; they had pictures in their wallets and stories to tell. Then, when the war shifted to the South Pacific after Pearl Harbor, all these sailors, airmen, and troops were processed through Southern California, where they saw these hot roadsters. Of course, hot rodding exploded as a teen craze and spread rapidly across the country at the end of the war, mainly because of this exposure.

No photo in my collection says "backyard builder" better than this one. Plus, it epitomizes the Depression Era genesis of rodding: build it yourself, from whatever you've got, using whatever else you can get. This 1930 A roadster is only a few years old (photo is dated July 21, 1938), but it already looks well used. The owner has chopped and raked the windshield, added 1932 bumpers, possibly a high-compression head on the stock four, and one chrome wheel cover on mismatched tires. This is just the start.

Because most of the photos in my collection came from the scrapbooks of early rodders, as well as later ones who are or were local to this area, yes, most of the street-driven rods shown here do have California plates. I wish I had more examples from other areas in the early postwar rod boom, but I haven't been able to collect them, and I don't think all that much exists. I'll be less geographically constrained in later chapters. Here's a good look at the first hop-ups on the streets where they ran, with the people who built and enjoyed them.

Not all modified early Fords, however, were proto-hot rods. Many coach-built or custom-bodied cars were created during the affluent 1920s. This much-customized, or "streamlined," 1929 Ford roadster was hand-built in the mid-1930s by George Du Vall, with help from a local body shop. He had a good job at Southern California Plating Company at the time. Not only did he make one of his signature V-windshields for it (with a padded "French Top," possibly by Amos Carson), but the fenders are reshaped. It has a solid hood, a 1932 Plymouth grille, Woodlites, chrome disc wheel covers, and custom bumpers. This is not a gow job. It's one of the first customs, followed shortly by the incomparable Southern California Plating Company 1935 Phaeton delivery he co-built with Frank Kurtis.

So what is this? First, it's a great photo taken on a remote hilltop in East Los Angeles. The 1932 Vicky is only three years old, and it was Bill Burke's first nice car. So instead of stripping it down, he has accessorized it with 1934 bumpers, a single Woodlite, chrome wheel covers on jumbo whitewalls, and other chrome trim. The fact that it was a closed car meant it wasn't hop-up material in the first place. Knowing Bill, this car was meant to chauffeur young ladies, not race on the dusty, dry lakes.

Hot Rod Gallery   39

At first I thought this was the same roadster seen in the back yard (page 37), but closer scrutiny shows it's a Deuce, decked out with accessories. It also wears a Road Rebels club plate No. 1, denoting that it's the president's car. It has a chopped and raked windshield, but the rest (1934 bumpers, pinstripes, whitewalls and wheel discs, spare tire, and mud flaps) make this roadster more of a "doll-up" than a hop-up. This car-to-car action photo was taken as they arrived on the Muroc lakebed.

"This car-to-car action photo was taken as they arrived on the Muroc lakebed."

Chapter Two *On the Street*

> "I'm not sure what he'd call it, but there's no doubt he was proud of it."

Talk about a cool photo, not to mention one cool guy. After graduating from Manual Arts High School, young Burke got a good job (despite the Depression) at the Goodrich tire plant, and saved enough to buy this 1936 three-window coupe brand new. Then he immediately went to Eastern Auto to buy accessories such as solid hood sides, fog lights, fender lights, and so on. I'm not sure what he'd call it, but there's no doubt he was proud of it.

Hot Rod Gallery 41

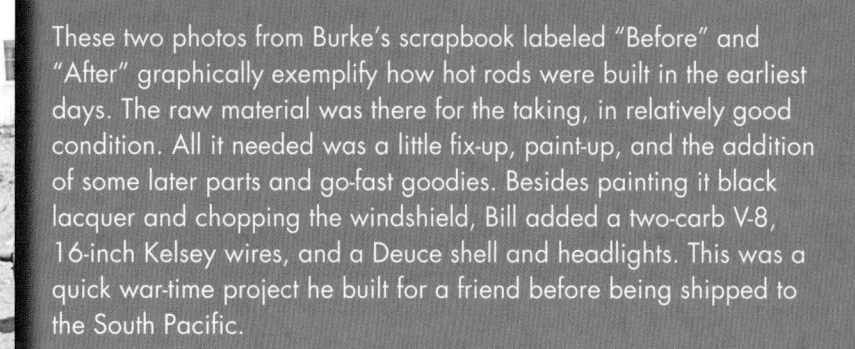

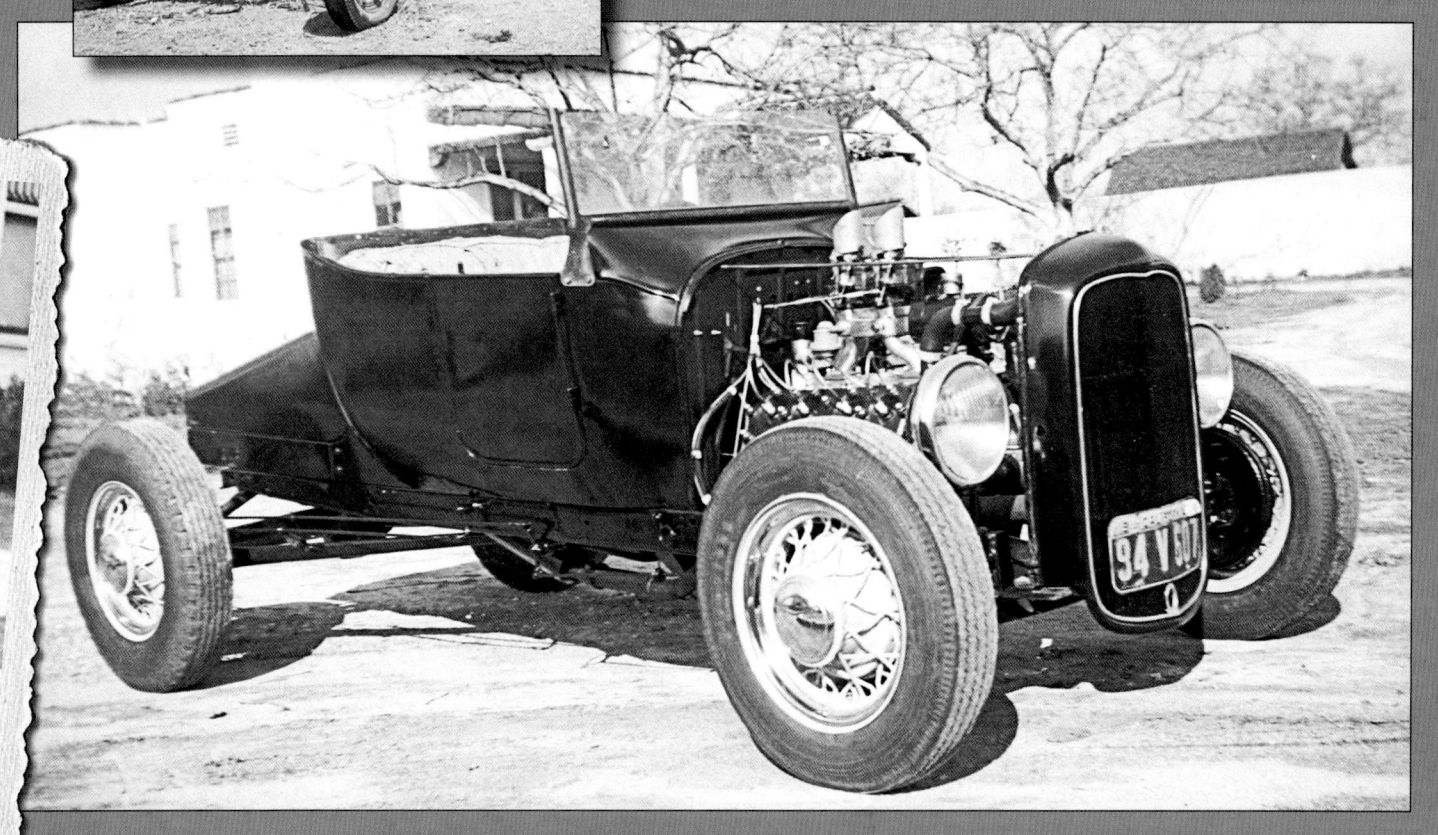

These two photos from Burke's scrapbook labeled "Before" and "After" graphically exemplify how hot rods were built in the earliest days. The raw material was there for the taking, in relatively good condition. All it needed was a little fix-up, paint-up, and the addition of some later parts and go-fast goodies. Besides painting it black lacquer and chopping the windshield, Bill added a two-carb V-8, 16-inch Kelsey wires, and a Deuce shell and headlights. This was a quick war-time project he built for a friend before being shipped to the South Pacific.

This picture tells a story, but I don't know what it is. I think the plate is from Texas. The otherwise stock, stripped T has a round tank on the back, chopped windshield, little tractor lights, and steel wheels with no front brakes. Is the guy in the background with a hat a cop writing a ticket? Who's the dude with the pipe? This is one more example that "T-Buckets" existed in a wide variety of forms on the street, lakes, and circle tracks.

One of the more curious and mysterious additions to my archive was a letter-size envelope bulging with 3 x 5 snapshots that a friend happened to see sitting in a trashcan, out at the sidewalk on trash day, in Pasadena. I have no idea who took the pictures, but he had a decent camera and pointed it at any modified vehicles he saw on the streets, in SoCal and other places. All are from around 1945, so possibly he was traveling in the service. There's some nice work and good parts (a two-carb, finned-head V-8 filled the Deuce shell) on this channeled 1929, but the filled and cut-down doors with puffy upholstery were strictly sports-car-ville, man.

Another channeled A from the "trashcan file" has a 1945 California plate, teardrop taillights, whitewalls with ripple discs, a handmade V-windshield above a dash full of gauges, split front wishbones, and a solid hood with a strange, single, small exhaust pipe. It's painted and upholstered. Somebody put a lot of work into this street roadster. Classic? No. Typical? Maybe . . . more or less.

Hot Rod Gallery 43

What appear to be classic hot rods to us today were often just "quickies." Today, we'd call this Deuce hiboy traditional. All Bill Burke did was strip parts off this 1932 roadster, add two carbs on the 21-stud V-8, and bolt on some headlights, taillights, and Kelsey wires with big-and-little tires. That's it. He did it on home-leaves during the war. It looks great.

Here's another great backyard-building scene, titled "Joe Rethy's First A-V-8," and dated July 12, 1938. That means this 1930–1931 Sport Coupe is only a few years old. Yet someone very neatly chopped the top a couple inches sometime before this. It shows that all early hop-ups didn't have to be roadsters.

Chapter Two On the Street

So what did the first "roadster boys" look like? Both Bill Burke and future *Throttle* Publisher/Editor Jack Peters belonged to a club called the Road Rebels that was associated with the Western Timing Association. They wore their club name on the back of white overalls, similar to those worn by crews at Indy and other big car races. And they really did wear those white "Stroker caps."

They also cleaned up pretty well, as seen in this photo where they're displaying their hand-painted club "plate" that predated cast-aluminum "plaques." That's tall Peters standing in the middle, with Burke to his right. They might be called Road Rebels, but they look like pretty wholesome American boys.

On the road the Road Rebels appear to be a fun-loving group, even when the ignition craps out on their four-year-old, front-fenderless 1936 three-window coupe on the long drive up Mint Canyon on the way to Muroc. This scrapbook photo is titled "Refreshments."

That 1938 DeLuxe convertible sedan has to be nearly new (but already fitted with skirts, flippers, and spotlights . . . and one missing taillight), so who knows why they're stopped at this highway junction in the high desert somewhere near Palmdale. Or what they're doing. But they're obviously having fun (a basic element of hot rodding), and it makes for another amazing photograph.

Hot Rod Gallery   45

You may have seen this picture before, but it's too good to leave out. Yes, street racing, usually impromptu like this, was an inevitable fact of hot rodding's genesis. It's an intrinsic element of automotive history. But how many photos have you seen of it actually happening? Who took this photo? Well, Burke told me it was on Slauson Avenue, between Figueroa and Hoover "right in front of my house." Jack Peters caught Bill's stripped 1929 A-V-8 just ahead of Paul Speirs' shinier one in 1939 or 1940. Yes, it was sort of set up. This is from the original scratchy negative.

"Yes, street racing, usually impromptu like this, was an inevitable fact of hot rodding's genesis."

46 Chapter Two On the Street

The well-known black 1927 T with the high-mounted side pipes from its big 1941 Cadillac flathead V-8 is Connie Weidell's, and I've always liked this photo of all the young guys checking it out at the curb. The strange part is that it had mufflers, but no lights or windshield. Then I found the other angle, showing more "spectators" at a gas station across the street, as well as on the new 1940 Dodge hood. Other photos showed more race cars at the station. This was an "organized," although still clandestine and somewhat impromptu, street race.

Hot Rod Gallery 47

This is another photo I've long wondered about. It's the Caruthers car, wearing its lakes number, but it's on the street. Art Chrisman told me Doug actually added headlights and a windshield and licensed the car for the street. You can see the windshield still in place. It's apparent he's here for some sort of race, not cruising. Not much could beat this light, little Modified from a dead start (as Chrisman proved on drag strips later). We've all heard tales about rodders bringing all-out race cars to street drags. Well, here's photographic evidence.

"It's apparent he's here for some sort of race, not cruising."

Here's another of my favorite photos from Burke's box. Yes, there were bare-bones, primered roadsters in the mix. This one has no windshield (hence the goggles) or grille. It has mechanical brakes because Ford didn't introduce hydraulics until that year: 1939. Details such as the filled cowl and generally tidy workmanship indicate that this work in progress will one day be nicely finished.

This scratchy photo has its own story. It's wartime. This young sailor finally gets leave to come home for a few days, and he's been parted from his hot rod for so long he can't resist getting it out and firing it up for a hot lap or two around the block, even though this Whippet-grille, Cragar-head Modified is obviously not street legal. Hey, the lakes were closed for the war. The story might not be true, but that's what this picture says to me.

48 Chapter Two *On the Street*

Another common wartime scenario was the younger brother borrowing the big brother's roadster while he was gone in the service. The cute redhead in the two-piece was my mother's friend Dorothy, posing with her boyfriend's (brother's) 1930 A-V-8 in front of the famous Rendezvous Ballroom at Balboa Beach in 1943 or 1944.

With this photo Dorothy noted they were "getting a ticket for loud pipes" near Santa Ana High, where they went to school. Again, who took the photo? Note the rock behind the rear wheel.

I was able to contact older brother Al Voegtely, who sent me more photos. In this one he's looking plenty tough from his wartime hitch, now home and already at work further modifying his Model A with steel wheels, a recessed license plate, and his Clutchers club plaque on the deck lid. By the time the nearby Santa Ana Drag Strip opened in 1950, it had a full-race 1946 Merc and was stripped for track action exclusively.

Hot Rod Gallery   49

This was some sort of press photo released by the Los Angeles Police Department (the sign he's pasting in the window says "traffic violator"). This is the type of car that made "hot rod" a bad name and engendered the wrath of cops just after the war. The driver looks as if he's being persecuted, but his T-V-8 not only has wire wheels, mechanical brakes, a stupidly mounted battery, and no grille, but it's also shoddily built and filthy. It would have been called a "shot rod" (or worse) in 1947.

> "This is the type of car that made 'hot rod' a bad name and engendered the wrath of cops just after the war."

50 Chapter Two *On the Street*

It's not a great photo, but Bob Schull's abbreviated street T-V-8 is an excellent example of the breed from the mid-1940s. It doesn't have much chrome, but it appears painted and upholstered, with nice side pipes, bullet headlights, what looks like a rounded tractor-type grille, a single taillight below a club plaque, and a perfect set of big-and-little tires.

"Need more proof that T-Buckets were common long before Grabowski and Ivo?"

Need more proof that T-Buckets were common long before Grabowski and Ivo? Best of all, just like their cars (and unlike all the fiberglass "kit car" copies of the 1970s), each one seemed to have its own shape, slant, and personality. This one, seen in 1949 or 1950, is not only long and low, but has a much molded, slightly narrowed Dodge body with a matching cut-down windshield, along with a cut-down 1932 Ford grille.

Hot Rod Gallery 51

This is a very cool photo of a totally cool and talented guy. Gus Maanum was the artist who drew the ink sketches of dust-spewing race cars that graced the covers of SCTA programs in the 1940s. And not only did he ride this immaculately detailed black 1941 Harley 61, but he also had a similarly black and beautiful full-fendered 1932 roadster that was featured at the 1949 SCTA Hot Rod Exposition.

Duffy Livingstone was an early rodder, partner with Dave Mitchell in his Pasadena muffler shop, builder-driver of the famous *Eliminator* 1923 T road racer, and founder of the Go-Kart Company, among many other kudos. He didn't have the best camera, but he took lots of hot rod photos, and shared about three full albums with me. This is a snapshot he took of two roadsters on a Pasadena neighborhood street in the 1940s. The thing I love about it is the youth and exuberance of the kids in them. Check out the chopped, raked windshield on the 1932.

I hate the overused word "icon," but Doane Spencer was one in the annals of hot rodding, as was his slick, black 1932 roadster, seen here in the lineup of cars taking off from the Rose Bowl on the 1947 Pasadena Reliability Run, where it was presented the trophy (by Wally Parks and Ak Miller) for Best Appearing Car. I was privileged to have known Doane, and he had a whole drawer full of loose photos he let me borrow.

Among the photos in Duffy's albums were several showing the complete build-up of Dave Mitchell's excellent Olds-powered 1929 roadster pickup, lettered to advertise the muffler shop. It not only won the 1948 Reliability Run, but was also featured in an early *HRM*. I like this portrait of the finished car partly because of what's in the background: a woody, a shoebox, and Little Lulu advertising Kleenex.

Hot Rod Gallery 53

Veteran/pioneer hot rodder Frank Currie took lots of pictures in the early days, mostly in Orange County (south of Los Angeles). These two are significant, not only because they show a great lineup of fenderless roadsters, but they also show that "rod runs" have been part of the mix since the early days. These are members of the Strokers club from Whittier, who have cruised down to Irvine Park in Santa Ana on a chilly winter day in 1947. Frank was quick to emphasize that "They all ran the lakes, too" come summer.

> "I can only assume these happy guys are fellow members of the Vultures club."

Here's another good one from George Bentley's cigar box. I can only assume these happy guys are fellow members of the Vultures club from East Los Angeles sometime in the latter 1940s. Although Joe Nitti isn't one of them, there's a slight chance that this good-looking Deuce hiboy is the one that later became famous as his. Maybe.

It would be considered sexist today, but this publicity photo touted the fact that Marcia Campbell was the "only girl" with a car entered in the first Hot Rod Exposition. Although she was later known for a couple of very nice Barris customs of her own, and her photographs of others, her 1929 roadster pickup, as shown here, hardly looks like it would qualify. My guess is that she got a quickie Barris paint job and a new windshield before the show opened.

Hot Rod Gallery   55

Is this a car show? No. The roadster craze was so strong in the late 1940s that D&B Auto Sales in Hollywood not only filled its lot with rods and customs, but they even placed memorable Tom Medley–illustrated ads in 1948–1949 issues of *HRM*. If you look closely at this photo (back, center), you can just barely see the top of Ralph Schenck's lakes streamliner, which was for sale that day.

The gorgeous Eddie Dye track roadster, built by the Ayala brothers with a nose, hood, and belly pans by Whitey Clayton and an engine by Earl Evans, got virtually no publicity beyond the black-and-white March 1952 cover of *Hop Up* and feature inside. I got this excellent photo directly from George Du Vall, whose V-windshield was part of the package. Surprisingly, it still exists and is currently being restored.

> "Surprisingly, this gorgeous Eddie Dye track roadster still exists and is currently being restored."

We're obviously entering a new era here. It's 1953. Hot rodding is no longer a teen craze, and the name has even taken on a more respectable meaning. This young couple are making their way in more affluent times with a new house, nice clothes, and a very clean red 1934 roadster wearing wide whitewalls, Merc wheels, and a full hood and fenders. Very classy. That's a term that couldn't have been applied to a hop-up or gow job a decade or two earlier.

Talk about pictures telling a story, there's a lot going on in this one from George Du Vall. That's probably driver Clyde Sturdy working on the SoCal belly tank outside the Western Motel in Wendover; that's his Associated Gear pickup hooked to the trailer. That's Dr. and Mrs. Wetzel in the channeled, yellow, V-windshield roadster stopping to chat and check it out. You might notice a small trailer on the back of the roadster but you can't see the Missouri license plates. The channeled 1932 was largely built by Valley Custom in Burbank, then bought and finished by Dr. Leland Wetzel in Springfield, Missouri, who then drove it, with his wife and another couple in another topless roadster, to Bonneville and back for the 1952 Meet. The adventure was chronicled by Mrs. Wetzel in a three-page story in the December 1952 *HRM*.

Hot Rod Gallery   57

"It's 1953 and things have certainly changed since the days of double-duty lakes/street roadsters, haven't they?"

It's 1953 and things have certainly changed since the days of double-duty lakes/street roadsters, haven't they? It's very likely this clean-cut, smiling young couple have never driven off pavement, nor heard of clubs with names like Vultures or Knight Riders. Look at all that shiny chrome on the dropped-axle front end. It has excellent bodywork, paint, white upholstery, and even small fenders. New magazines and the advent of organized, judged car shows in 1950 had a lot to do with it; hot rodders had pretty successfully shed their outlaw image.

It's a shame this isn't in color, but of the many photos Tom Pollard had of this car, such as this one posed on the street of his hometown Monterey Park, all were black-and-white. Having first appeared in red with a yellow four-carb flathead on the August 1954 *Rod & Custom (R&C)* cover, it next made the *HRM* cover in January 1955 with *Dragnet*'s Jack Webb. Then Barris painted this car lime green with Honduras Maroon crab-claw flames; he painted George Sein's Deuce coupe with similar flames, but in the reverse color scheme. Then he had Von Dutch and Dean Jeffries stripe them together during the 1954 Motorama show, and they both appeared, thus emblazoned, on the "little" June 1957 *Car Craft* cover, one of the wildest ever. I located and showed the current state of both cars in my recent book, *Lost Hot Rods*.

"I've presented this photo in the past to answer the perpetual reader inquiry, 'How do I get my car in your magazine?'"

Hot Rod Gallery   59

Again, this photo should be in color, because the wild and crude red/orange/yellow flames on the front of Bob McCoy's otherwise stock-bodied 1940 sedan are one of the first and best examples of "customizing with paint," perfected by Larry Watson ten years later. In fact, the buffed black on the rest of the body is factory original. This photo shows that striper/artist/racer McCoy was at least as dynamic and colorful as his car. He still is today. Sadly, this classic rod has been restored to a stone stocker.

I've presented this photo in the past to answer the perpetual reader inquiry, "How do I get my car in your magazine?" Like this. Gary McCann's Pontiac-powered 1932 five-window is nice, but nothing exceptional other than being channeled with full fenders. However, when he parked the Maidenformed lady next to it, snapped some pictures, and sent them to R&C, sure enough, they featured it in the September 1960 issue.

CHAPTER THREE

The First Car Shows

We call them custom car shows today. You might be surprised that the very first rod-and-custom shows were called roadster shows, hot rod exhibitions, or hot rod expositions, and their express purpose was to demonstrate to a disapproving public that these homebuilt, fast, often noisy cars were in fact safe, well-engineered, and even beautiful.

Even though it wasn't a static car show, per se, I start with the Pasadena Reliability Run in 1947 because its express purpose was to demonstrate to the public, the police, and the press that these cars could easily travel more than 100 miles to the top of 7,000-foot mountains and back, do it safely, and observe all speed limits along the way. The sponsoring group had even taken the name Pasadena Roadster Club, rather than Throttlers, Trompers, Stokers, or Velociteers to distance such modified cars from the decidedly negative image the newspapers had already bestowed on hot rods. This 1947 run was actually a progenitor of 1970s rod runs. It also included a gathering in the grassy Rose Bowl parking lot where a trophy was awarded to the Best Appearing Car: Doane Spencer's outstanding black Deuce.

By 1948 the Southern California Timing Association (SCTA), the organization uniting dozens of clubs throughout Southern California that raced at the dry lakes, took a different approach. They decided to stage a large indoor show in the National Guard Armory in Exposition Park in Los Angeles (next to the Coliseum, at the site of the 1932 Olympics) and, after much heated discussion, decided to call it the Hot Rod Exposition. This was an outright example of grabbing the bull by the horns. The newspapers had turned the term "hot rod" into a pejorative, akin to "biker gang," and the show's dedicated purpose was to turn that image around.

The organizers wanted the public to see how wrong its perception of "hot rods" was. The show included street-driven roadsters, all-out lakes racers, and at least one Barris custom, in addition to several manufacturers' booths displaying shiny, well-engineered parts. There were no judging or trophies at this show; just being selected by the SCTA to appear, from the hundreds that applied, was honor enough. Some 55,000 people paid to attend. It was eminently successful, both in its stated purpose and in establishing hot rod car shows.

It also directly motivated Bob Petersen to print the first issue of *Hot Rod Magazine*, but that's a long story in itself. What surprises me is that it took until 1948 for the SCTA (or anyone else) to stage a show like this, that it only lasted two years, and that we have so little photographic evidence or records of it today.

"The organizers wanted the public to see how wrong its perception of 'hot rods' was."

The first big (and longest lasting) commercial hot rod car show was, of course, the Oakland Roadster Show. On the occasion of that show's Fortieth Anniversary, I stated on the cover of *Rod & Custom (R&C)* in June 1989 that the first one was held in 1949, and that the wonderful trove of 4 x 5 black-and-white negatives given to me by

Eric Rickman for the story inside were from that show. He said they were. Others did too. Confusion arises from the fact that Al Slonaker held a car show across the Bay in 1949, and did include some roadsters as a "test" to see if the public would go for it.

However, the first National Roadster Show with the giant trophy for America's Most Beautiful Roadster (won by Bill Niekamp's 1929 track-nose) was in January 1950. . . I'm pretty sure. The best part is that Oakland native Rickman took well over 100 photos of the show as a freelancer (leading directly to his life-long career at Petersen Publications), and gave them to me to keep in 1989. The one thing that still puzzles me, however, is why there is no photo of the Niekamp car among these negs, not even in the background, and I've never seen one printed of it at this show. I've seen photos of it the following year, propped up on hay bales, with the big trophy next to it. I don't know. And Rick's no longer here to ask.

This brings up a final point for this chapter, and the whole book for that matter. Although I've grouped photos into relevant, chronological categories, this is by no means a comprehensive history of hot rodding. This is a gallery of some of the best photos in my large collection. I can only show the photos I have. I wish I had good

Yes, this is a double exposure. Those of you raised on motor-drive SLRs and digital cameras might never have seen one. They were common in the old days, especially with large-format cameras, when you had to manually rewind, or change, the film for each new photo. This was to be an overall "lead photo" taken by freelancer Eric Rickman at the first Oakland Roadster Show. As usual, he had found a place to get a high angle, mounting his big 4 x 5 Speed Graphic on a tripod for a timed exposure. Except that he forgot to change the film before snapping the second picture. The shot simply multiplies the crowd, the banners, and all the shiny cars unfettered by ropes or stanchions. It looks fun, popular, exciting, and set the tone for decades of car shows to come.

photos of the Indy Car Show and the Detroit Autorama for this chapter, for instance, also begun in the very early 1950s. In fact I have several from the first Indy show, but neither the photos or the cars in them are good.

The point is that I'm selecting photos that I think are great, for one reason or another, from the ones I happen to have. They're representative, to be sure, but don't expect them to be comprehensive. That's not the idea. Enjoy what's here; I think you will.

The Pasadena Roadster Club held its first Reliability Run in 1947, beginning and ending at the well-known Rose Bowl, traversing the hazy mountains in the background. Records are sketchy but the event ran about five years. These cars are lined up for a cold, misty, early-morning start in 1949 or 1950, judging from one shoebox Ford in the background. The 1929 roadster in the foreground has a Trompers of Eagle Rock plaque. The nice Deuce roadster on the left is one of the few with whitewalls. And it's interesting that there are several coupes in the mix.

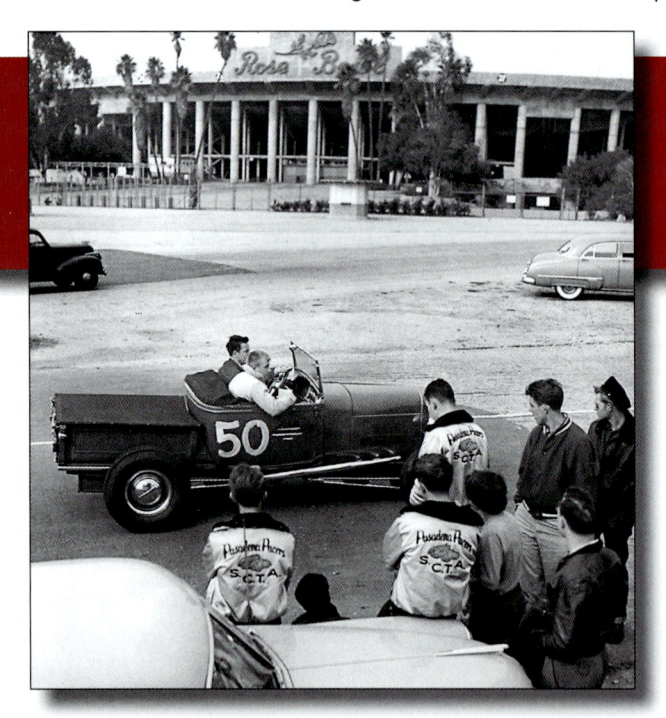

> "Photos from the first two (and only) SCTA Hot Rod Expositions are scarce, and I only have a few."

You saw Dave Mitchell's Olds-powered roaster pickup in Chapter Two on page 52. It reportedly won the first Pasadena run, coming closest to the pre-set "correct" elapsed time; this might be a later year. That's his muffler shop partner Duffy Livingstone as "navigator." I love the composition of this photo with the satin club jackets in the foreground and the Rose Bowl in the distance, plus the way he's poster-painted the number on the door.

Photos from the first two (and only) SCTA Hot Rod Expositions are scarce, and I only have a few. This one of the Burke & Francisco belly tank has to be from the 1949 show because the poster lists a World's Fastest Time of 153.32 mph, which was set in August 1948. It also wears No. 3 (not Sweet 16) and a three-tone purple/lavender paint scheme seen on the August 1949 *HRM* cover. Many cars around the perimeter were tilted on blocks, like this. Note the absence of an engine (no exhaust pipes), but the addition of fancy wheel covers for the show.

Hot Rod Gallery 63

This excellent photo was taken by Sacramento Thunderbolts member Norm Milne, the only one that "came out" of several he took on his trip to the first SCTA show. That's why we have so few indoor or nighttime photos from that era; the lighting was iffy, especially for amateurs. I know virtually nothing about Dan Busby, the Dolphins, or this beautiful 1927 T roadster, other than Marvin Webb of Orange County probably built it, as you will see in Chapter Six on page 30.

This photo is definitely from the 1948 show because Bob McGee's smooth red Deuce was one of the featured cars selected to appear, as it did on the October 1948 *HRM* cover. There were no trophies or judging. The SCTA chose fifty to eighty (depending on the source) of the best hot rods then available to show the public that they weren't hoodlum-owned jalopies.

Chapter Three The First Car Shows

The following five photos are a mini-story I've been trying to sort out for years. Bill Burke told me about the car, and had one large, mounted photo. Recently I acquired more through *Rodder's Journal* contributor Jay Fitzhugh, who got them from a former Kinmont Brake employee. Here's the deal: At the first show, which lasted just three days, a 1932 hiboy roadster was built on stage by a small team headed by Lou Baney and including Bill Burke. At the second nine-day show two roadsters were built, one by a Baney-led team (painted orange) and the other by a Burke-led team (painted Burple). All three finished rods were raffled off as door prizes. The trouble is trying to tell which shows/cars the photos depict. I think this is the 1948 show, at the start. The "before" car appears to have been a fenderless lakes competitor, given the faded number on the door. You can see the work stage is right in the show. That's Burke in the middle talking to the crowd. Dig the toolboxes.

I don't see Baney in any of these photos, but this primered car might be the orange one. What's amazing about this photo are the gennie parts, especially the cherry front fender, which were taken off and tossed.

> "The following five photos are a mini-story I've been trying to sort out for years."

This must be the 1949 show because the sign lists the crew as Bill Burke, Rulon Gregor, and Harvey Haller. Bill told me they painted the cars on stage, after show hours. Parts such as the chromed dropped axle and Kinmont disc brakes were supplied by vendors at the show. I assume the engine on the left is the stocker, with the hot new one being assembled on the right.

Hot Rod Gallery 65

This is the photo I got from Burke, who's on the right, as his purple car nears completion in 1949. As you can see, they were nice cars, especially with the polished Kinmont brakes. I had the names of all three winners, and tried tracing the cars, but didn't get very far. What do you suppose happened to them?

This is a classic photo. That's the Kinmont Manufacturing Company in the background, and those perky ladies were two handy secretaries. This is the 1948 Giveaway car (won by Nelson C. Morris of Long Beach). In a photo of this car in brief show coverage in the March 1948 *HRM*, it appears to be a somewhat lighter metallic color; here it looks black. No reports state what color the first car was.

In Oakland, California, across the Bay from San Francisco, long-time circle track race promoter Al Slonaker staged his first National Roadster Show January 19–22, 1950, in the Oakland Auditorium, promising "more than 100 roadsters from across the U.S." for this "spectacular exhibition-competition." While a few cars came from Sacramento, Reno, and Los Angeles, most were local, but of exceptionally high quality, such as these Bay Area track roadsters. Unlike the Pasadena and SCTA events, this show marked the beginning of car shows as commercial enterprises (or club fund-raisers), including competition among entrants for trophies in various classes.

You can see there are plenty of people, ropes to keep them at bay, and plenty of very nice roadsters on display. Check the early four-bar suspension on the T-V-8. The one at the rear had a Cadillac overhead V-16, and is still in the Oakland area.

Hot Rod Gallery 67

With chromed wheels, a completely chromed Deuce frame, and a chrome-drenched engine and firewall visible under a hand-formed Plexiglas hood, you would think Ken Fuhrman's black 1929 roadster was a competitive car-show veteran, built specifically to win trophies (as so many were later). But it couldn't have been. What's even more amazing is that Ken showed the same car, in exactly the same condition, at the 40th Anniversary show in 1989, and still owns it.

> "The steerhide tuck-and-roll upholstery, fortunately, didn't catch on."

The orange scallops and white pinstripes on Don Rocci's 1927 T roadster pickup are the handiwork of Tommy "The Greek" Hrones, and became a Bay Area hot rod hallmark for decades to follow. The Deuce shell, three-piece hood, and belly pans are likely by equally legendary area metal-man Jack Haggeman. The steerhide tuck-and-roll upholstery, fortunately, didn't catch on.

Today, we'd call Robert Workman's 1932 hiboy traditional, but then it was contemporary. In fact, the padded, headlined, dark Hall's top might have been considered modern for the time. One side of the custom hood has been removed to display the much-chromed mill. The headlight stands are made from fender braces. Several of these Bay Area rods had nerf bars, like these, influenced by the popular track roadsters.

68   Chapter Three   *The First Car Shows*

Whether Owen Greenan's little four-pot-powered T-Bucket was influenced by Tom Medley's *Stroker McGurk* cartoons in *HRM*, or vice versa, is hard to say. Both were highly influenced by the track roadsters of the era, even though this one is strictly built for the street. Just one more example of the early evolution of the T-Bucket style.

Stuart Hilborn obviously (and fortunately) kept his first fuel injection unit when he sold his gorgeous, famous, record-breaking "streamliner" to the Grant Piston Ring Company to use for promotion. That's why it also has a clear plastic hood to show off its 21-stud V-8 refitted with its Eddie Miller mismatched four-carb setup.

> "From the beginning, Eric Rickman couldn't pass up the chance to pose a smiling blonde with a car he was photographing."

From the beginning, Eric Rickman couldn't pass up the chance to pose a smiling blonde with a car he was photographing, and the 1950 Oakland show queen was happy to oblige. George Pacheco's equally good-looking, painted, upholstered, and chromed track T was also highly competitive, displaying the big 1947 NCRRA Championship trophy, among others.

Hot Rod Gallery 69

This appears to be made from a 1947–1948 Studebaker convertible, possibly as a factory show car (featured in an early *Motor Trend*). I present it here primarily to show that the first bubble-top custom wasn't built by Roth or Starbird. It's also interesting to note how many men are wearing hats, ties, or coats, and the fact that trashcans seemed to be non-existent.

A very young-looking, but already quite successful, George Barris brought about six of his customs up from Los Angeles for the show, including Don Vaughn's Cadillac-finned, Carson-topped 1947 Buick behind him. The smiling girl on the right is the show queen. The lady on the left, George told me when I showed him the photo, "Is my aunt Edith, who raised me and Sam as a loving 'mother' who gave us a very good life." From nearby Roseville, she came to visit George at the show.

Chapter Three: The First Car Shows

Taking a cue from the successful SCTA shows, Slonaker also arranged to have a roadster "built" at his first show. Bob DeBisschop's under-construction 1929 roadster was hurriedly painted, chromed, and upholstered (by Hall's Top Shop), then disassembled in the Ben Hubbard Auto Parts booth, to be reassembled by a young crew in white coveralls during the four-day show.

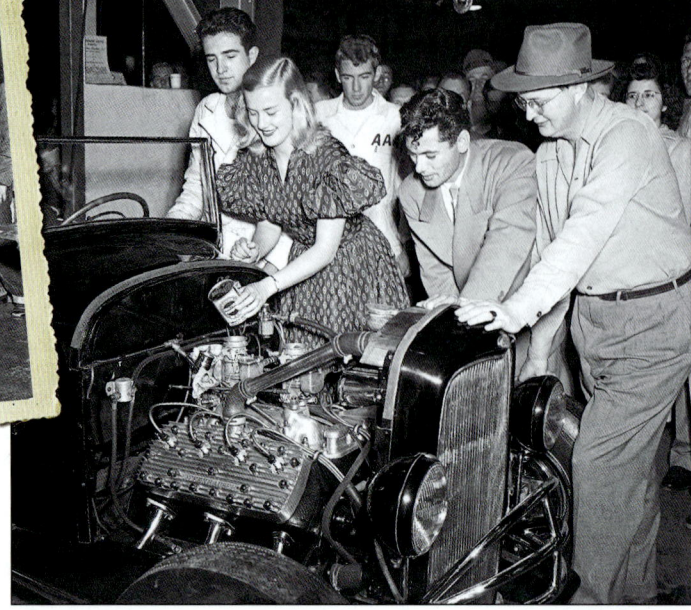

With hotshot local circle track driver Freddie Agabashian at her side, the still-smiling show queen pours in a quart of Wynn's Friction Proofing before the finished car was fired up on the final night, to the crowd's joy.

You've probably seen a well-known photo of a similar one-day parking lot car show including several famous customs and rods of the early 1950s. You don't see any famous cars at this one hosted by the Lords car club of Wilmington around 1953, but this is one of those photos you just want to study. You see some trophies waiting to be handed out. Because it's a free show, it must have been done at the club's expense, just for fun and mutual admiration. Such shows were precursors to ever-popular cruise nights and more recent early-morning donut meets.

Hot Rod Gallery 71

Having seen the huge success of the first two SCTA shows (the second drawing 60,000 spectators) and experienced the phenomenal growth of *HRM* and his budding publishing empire, Robert E. Petersen was quick to step in with his own Motorama shows when SCTA bowed out. Staging the first one in the Los Angeles Shrine Auditorium in 1950, then moving to the fabulous, Streamline Moderne Pan Pacific Auditorium for the next four years, these were highly promoted, very commercial affairs. Not only were the walls and aisles hung with large drapes and signage, but also cars were set off in booths lined with planters filled with shrubbery (real or artificial?). I believe this is the 1950 show, where Barris had several Kustoms prominently displayed, including Dan Landon's very chopped 1949 Chevy coupe.

This is well before the age of angel hair, but it appears to be white crushed gravel on the floor with fitted wood banisters around the perimeter of Art and Jack Chrisman's stunning, Dutch-striped race cars at the 1954 Motorama. As far as I know, these displays were constructed and provided by Petersen. Running at least five days and nights, these shows were a totally different experience than the parking lot type. And they weren't free.

Chapter Three *The First Car Shows*

Having just been rebodied and painted by the Chrismans before the 1954 Motorama, the Reed Brothers Hemi-powered tank not only displayed more chrome than most lakesters, but also one of Von Dutch's more extravagant works of art, including lettering, striping, wild flames, and a "weirdo" of a man-baby riding a flying eyeball on the nose.

> "As a teen, I'd heard an urban legend that Von Dutch had 'gone crazy' and pinstriped an entire car, inside and out, at some big car show."

Andy Southard took this rare color photo of the Yeakel Brothers Cadillac-powered lakes roadster, followed by its matching F-100 push truck, at the 1955 Motorama. This shows more of Dutch's amazing work, including the notorious upside-down monster head in the grille, as well as a combination of white rock, wood rail, and potted shrubbery in the then-elaborate display.

As a teen, I'd heard an urban legend that Von Dutch had "gone crazy" and pinstriped an entire car, inside and out, at some big car show. Later, I'd heard him claim that Petersen had somehow coerced him into striping one car in a display booth for ten days. Then, as I was finishing a book on Dutch ten years ago, I found two photos supposedly showing him just starting the job at the 1955 Motorama. This enlargement, showing the dressy punk couple in the background, not to mention the guy with his foot on the rail, well, tells a story, don't it?

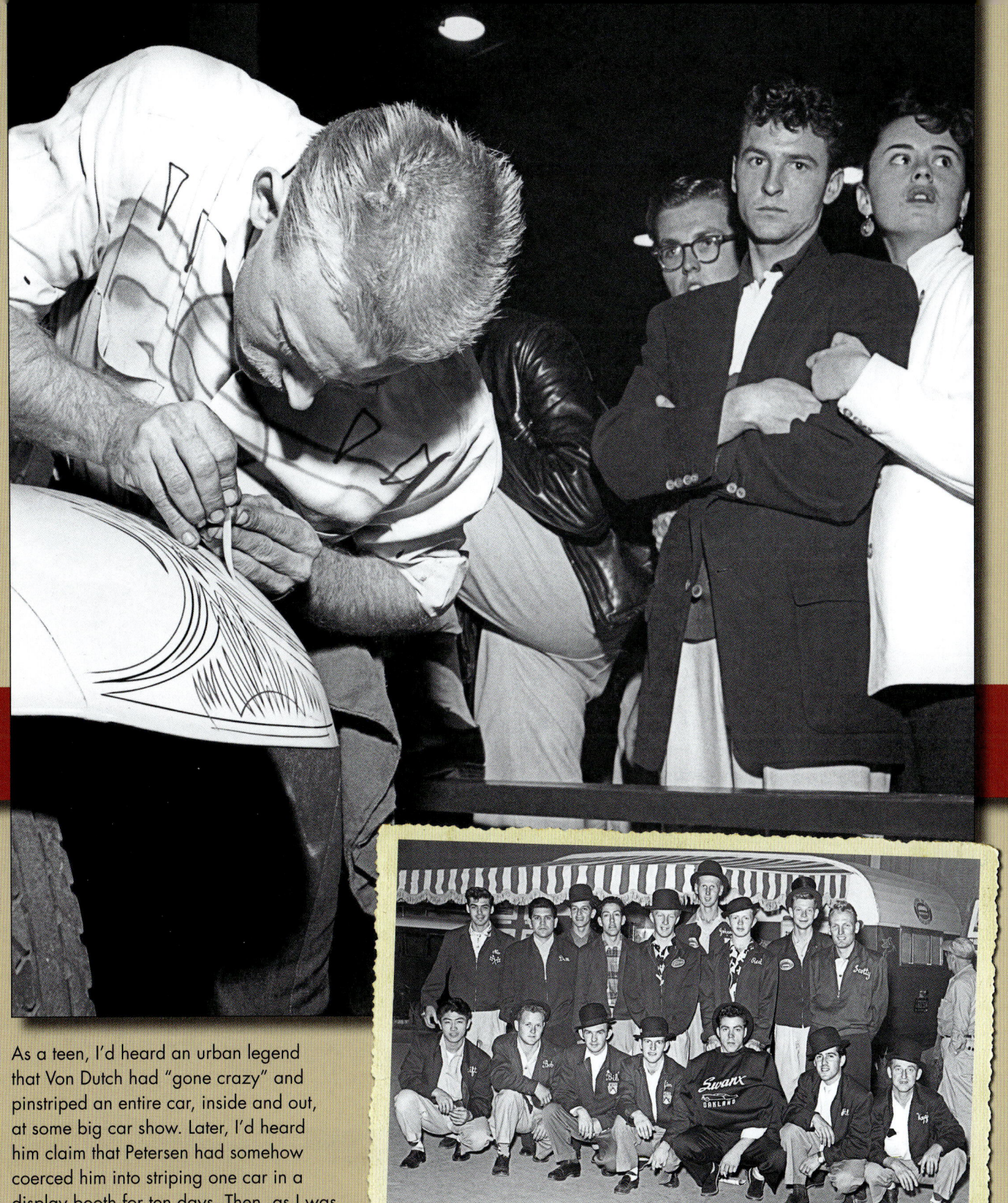

When I came across this photo a few years ago, I knew I had to add it to my collection. I forget who had it, and I had no idea how I might use it, but here it is, and it's cool. A note on the back of the original print just said "1954 Motorama." That's the SCTA Drag Safari trailer in the background. The Swanx of Oakland was revived as a retro tribute club about five years ago.

Chapter Three *The First Car Shows*

Another type of popular car show in the early 1950s was staged at new-car dealerships, this one at Les Bacon and Sons Ford in Hermosa Beach, California, in 1954. I suppose the rationale was that (especially on weekends, when mechanics' bays used to be closed) there was plenty of paved parking area, and inviting young guys interested in cars to spend a day at the dealership would introduce them to new Fords, and maybe someday they'd buy one. Nevertheless, being free and easily visible from the street, it was probably just another publicity stunt to get anybody to "come on down" to the dealership. As you can see from this sampling, show cars ranged from rods to customs to antiques; any make, even in primer.

There are tons of photos of Jesse Lopez' dark metallic green 1941 Ford, but this is my favorite. Built in 1946, this is the quintessential Barris custom of that early era. George even tried to patent the 1948 Cadillac grille installation! Given the number of clones of the Matranga 1940 Merc, I'm amazed this car hasn't been copied, imitated, or found and restored. Actually, I'm surprised to see it at this show in 1954, looking good, because Jesse said he had to sell it when he went to Korea. George told me Danny Lares of Wilmington bought it in 1953. Where did it go after that?

Hot Rod Gallery 75

Here's one close to my heart. It's Ike Iacono's beautiful, much-chromed, orange and black, Von Dutch lettered and striped 1933 Ford coupe with a potent Wayne twelve-port GMC engine that made the January 1954 *HRM* cover. This would definitely draw spectators off the street. It was the predecessor to his sleeker, faster twelve-port dragster, which I now own.

> "This would definitely draw spectators off the street."

This excellent, Cragar-powered 1923 turtle-deck T roadster seen at the Bacon car show is unidentified. The older engine and partial belly pans under the T or A frame indicate that it might have been an older lakes racer converted to street use; unfortunately in 1954 most rodders would have just considered it "old-fashioned" and out of style. I'd kill for a roadster just like this today (metaphorically speaking, of course).

Chapter Three *The First Car Shows*

Here's my favorite kind of car show: held outside, on a single day, in the football or baseball field of a local high school. These were highly popular during the 1950s when there was lots of club activity and nearly all "show" cars were still street-driven. You could easily drive cars in and line them up; the green grass was a fine backdrop. Better, it was an enclosed area, so the organizing club could charge a small spectator fee to pay for trophies and add to their coffers. In addition, the school could profit by letting booster clubs set up food and beverage stands, as they did at ball games. This hazy, early-morning photo from Downey High, around 1954–1955, is another to study closely.

> "The guy handing him the camshaft 'award' is none other than Wally Parks."

This curious photo was taken for a local newspaper. A tag on the back says the partially completed Model A drag "car" is owned by Ron Scrima (long-time dragster chassis-builder), so I assume that's him in the seat. The engine, also incomplete, is the C-T Automotive hemi-head conversion seen on the May 1955 *HRM* cover. The guy handing him the camshaft "award" is none other than Wally Parks, acting as *HRM* editor or NHRA president?

Hot Rod Gallery 77

"Here's my favorite kind of car show: held outside, on a single day, in the football or baseball field of a local high school."

Custom-painted cars in green fields on a sunny day made for a colorful spectacle, so I wish I had more color photos of it, but few exist. This is then-Barris-painter Junior Conway's bronze 1950 Ford coupe in its final form (note painted and striped insets in the open doorjamb). I got this good color photo, along with many others, from Junior himself.

Junior climbed onto a nearby roof to get this high-angle color photo of a one-day parking lot show "At the Sears in Compton in 1956." It must be late 1956 because I see a few new 1957 cars. Of note in the foreground is a red, tri-power V-8 1954 Corvette, Bruce Giesler's pink (ex-Ayala) GMC pickup, and what Junior thinks was the first outing for the primered *R&C Dream Truck*. I think the big white arrow adds impact to the photo.

Now we're back at the Oakland Roadster Show, 1959. The leggy, smiling sweater girl perched "just so" makes for a perfect 1950s pin-up photo. Larry Selmer's definitely Kookie T, thrown together from several track-racing buddies' spare parts, has plenty of eye appeal of its own.

Hot Rod Gallery 79

"This one influenced some of the wilder Fad Ts to follow, for sure."

If this were color, you'd see the body is blue while the engine and chassis parts are bright yellow. Later Mickey Himsl got it, painted it gold and purple 'flake, got it on the cover of *R&C*, and won lots of street races with it. The five-gallon gas tank gave it the name *Moonshiner*. This one influenced some of the wilder Fad Ts to follow, for sure.

This and the accompanying color photos are pure serendipity. Tom Connors, a fellow street rod club member at the time, handed me an envelope full of color snapshots and said, "Here, you'd like these." He took them with his Brownie camera at a car show sponsored by Pasadena High School, but held at the Arcadia armory in 1958 or 1959. That's his white 1940 coupe on the right, which had a dual-quad Vette mill. The Fordor Deuce and A sedans on the left epitomize my favorite hot rod period: baby moons with beauty rims, medium whitewalls, white tuck-and-roll interior, white roof inserts (with a tuck-and-roll stripe), and even white tuck-and-roll running boards on the black car.

What's surprising about Tom's snapshots of this small, local, late-1950s armory car show is the variety of cars that were there. Yes, that's Tony LaMasa's green channeled 1932 from the Los Angeles Roadsters (and *The Adventures of Ozzie and Harriet* TV show). Next to it is the even more famous Dick Scritchfield/Bob McGee Deuce roadster when it was painted light yellow for a brief period.

80   Chapter Three *The First Car Shows*

Yes, Norm Grabowski's T, the real *Kookie Kar* from *77 Sunset Strip,* was there. This is the one often credited as being the first "Fad T" hot rod. That's not exactly right, but it was certainly the first with this wild, yet jaunty look. And the big question mark on the sign epitomized the late Norman's huge sense of humor.

Here's a glimpse of Ike Iacono's orange and black GMC dragster (in a rare show appearance). Next to it is the gorgeous John Geraghty blown-Olds drag T, *Grasshopper,* sans body for some reason. It, of course, became a Monogram model kit, and both cars made the *HRM* cover in 1959. In fact all five cars in this photo did at one time or another.

Hot Rod Gallery 81

"This is a super-rare photo of Ron Aguirre's ever-evolving *X-Sonic* Corvette well before it got its bubble top."

I close this car show chapter with an event you've probably never heard of. It was a one-time affair held in a large, grassy employee park somewhere on the grounds of Disneyland in Anaheim in 1959 or 1960. Roth's *Outlaw* and *Tweedy Pie* were there, along with Graboski's T. This is a super-rare photo of Ron Aguirre's ever-evolving *X-Sonic* Corvette well before it got its bubble top. Not only does it have Lancer wheel covers, tuck-and-roll coves, scoops in the stock top, and handmade fins with a rolled pan, but also the faded-panels-over-white-pearl paint job, applied by Ed Roth, lasted just this one day. I don't even know what color it was, but Ed and Ron agreed it was ugly, and redid it the next day. The F-100 in the background is John Zupan's, built by Barris and painted by Dean Jeffries.

CHAPTER FOUR

The First Drag Strips

Who staged the first drag race? Where? When? Nobody really knows, and it probably didn't even involve cars. Horses still race from a standing start at a "gate," and usually run a quarter mile (albeit an oval one). We know from several accounts that "drag" races were staged at early Muroc meets in the 1930s, often with several cars abreast on the wide, dusty desert. And of course there has always been plenty of street racing, as you saw in Chapter Two, whether semi-organized in remote areas, or impromptu from stoplight to stoplight.

Nobody really knows where the term "drag" racing comes from. The dictionary doesn't even attempt a guess at its etymology. Rodders conjecture it comes from racing on the town's "main drag," or the dare from one rodder to another: "C'mon, drag 'er out and let's see what she'll do." I've even had more than one old-timer tell me, "It comes from the sound two cars make when they take off side-by-side," but that makes no sense to me.

Another thing I can't quite understand is why drag racing, of all motorsports, draws so much attention, reminiscence, argument, and data both in print and now even more so on the Internet. Perhaps it's because drag racing is by definition quantifiable. It's empirical. Each race has one winner and one loser. Records are kept for elapsed time (ET) and MPH. There are class winners and usually a Top Eliminator of some sort. Furthermore, drag races were held much more often, usually weekly, at many more venues during its heyday. Car shows, for instance, were usually held once a year, with one big one, per season, per city.

It seems that most of this recorded and debated information centers on the frantic 1960s. That was the golden age of front-engine Fuelers, Gassers, Fuel Altereds, and the first flopper Funny Cars. I'll start well before that, and won't care much who went 140 or 150 mph first. I'm more concerned with the bare strips of tarmac where these first organized drag races were staged, and the ingenious vehicles the hot rodders created to compete in this new, standing-start, short-sprint type of competition. The dragster, as it came to be known, is one of the most graphic examples ever of form following function.

"The first 'organized' drags held on a regular basis were by a group called the Santa Barbara Acceleration Association (SBAA)."

First, however, I would like to try to dispel, once again, a couple of legends of drag racing history that have been repeated so often that many accept them as fact. We define early drag racing as two cars racing from a dead stop (or possibly rolling start), with a flag starter, side-by-side down a paved straight strip, for a distance of about one-quarter mile, at the end of which one is declared the winner (and, with any luck, timed in seconds). The first "organized" drags held on a regular basis were by a group called the Santa Barbara Acceleration Association (SBAA). They occurred on an abandoned World War II air force base attached to the airport in Goleta, California, just north of Santa Barbara, in late 1948 or early 1949.

If you want to know more about the history and organization of these drags, I wrote a 14-page article about them in *The Rodder's Journal* No. 14 in 1999. I also discussed the evolution of numerous early strips in a two-part series, "The Lost Dragstrips of Southern California," in *Hot Rod Magazine*, September and October 2003.

Here's the story in a nutshell: An airbase was built in Goleta during World War II, but abandoned shortly after. A small airport was developed on the southern portion, but the northern part, with several buildings and paved roads, was left vacant. Local rodders used these roads to tune up their cars, mostly on Sunday afternoons. A local racer/engine builder named Bob Joehnck along with members of the Motor Monarchs club approached the airport management (who controlled the area) to ask if they could have permission to hold regular drags races there, every other Sunday. The manager said yes, as long as they secured insurance, which they did. The one straight, narrow, paved road they decided to use was approximately a quarter-mile long; the finish line was a narrow bridge with just enough shut-down room to stop before reaching a

I wish I had better photos of the Saugus, California, drags, but not only were the races "amateur," so were any photographers present. Nevertheless, this image of two contestants in the fendered coupe class being staged attests that they were well organized. The flag starter at the line is wearing a dark jacket with his white SBAA patch, as are the members on the platform ready to time the winner with stopwatches and record his number.

---

locked gate. With flagmen at the start and finish lines, the winner was timed with a stopwatch.

These were the first organized, legal, regularly scheduled drag meets anywhere, as far as I can ascertain. The SBAA was a volunteer, amateur organization. Rules were minimal, although cars were inspected and a few deemed unsafe were turned away. There was no entry fee for racers (about 50) or spectators (100 or more), so the SBAA made an agreement with a portable hot dog stand owner; he paid them 10 percent of his profits, which covered trophies and insurance.

The story has often been told that a grudge race between Tom Cobbs' supercharged Model A and Fran Hernandez' nitro-fueled Deuce coupe, known as the "Edelbrock car," was the first drag race.

There's another printed account of someone else being the first Top Eliminator there. Well, Goleta didn't have a Top Eliminator. It presented trophies to eliminations winners in three classes: Roadster, Coupe, and Full-Fendered Coupe/Sedan. That's why Cobbs built a removable steel top for his '29 roadster: He could race in either class (or both). His GMC-blown flathead won

84 Chapter Four *The First Drag Strips*

frequently. I don't know how or when the grudge race was arranged between Cobbs and Hernandez. They came up from Los Angeles on a scheduled race day (because it was the only legal place to do it) and raced once; Hernandez won as Cobbs spun his tires. Then Vic Edelbrock, Hernandez, and the team left for home as the regular races continued.

The SBAA Goleta drags petered out around 1951, mainly because other tracks opened, and the track's volunteers had to do everything, including cleaning up the trash. As for the first commercial drag strip operating on a regular basis, that was the legendary Santa Ana Drag Strip, opened in June 1950. C. J. Hart, Creighton Hunter, and Frank Stillwell (who had some motorcycle racing insurance) found an unused taxi strip parallel to the runway at the then-remote Santa Ana airport. First charging fifty cents to run, then a dollar, it paid ten percent of the profits to the airport, and made money through 1959.

Enough of these facts and history. Let's see what these seminal drag strips and racers looked like.

> "This is very early Santa Ana drags, when they gave cars a rolling start down a short incline to try to reduce parts breakage."

This is just a *good* photo. A young SBAA official brings Jack Quentin's good-looking Deuce three-window to the line. He had the top insert taped down so it wouldn't blow off; the side windows must have been taped more for effect.

This is very early Santa Ana drags, when they gave cars a rolling start down a short incline to try to reduce parts breakage. Being in a more populous area and running weekly, Santa Ana was where you saw all sorts of cars modified strictly for drags. This included a variety of classes, sometimes accommodated quickly with cardboard and masking tape, such as the Doodle Bug "coupe" on the right, made from a 1923 roadster.

As you can tell from the altered numbers and El Mirage dust in this soft-focus George Bentley photo, there were still plenty of cars that ran both lakes and drags in the early 1950s. If they had a quick-change to swap gears, they were lucky.

Chapter Four *The First Drag Strips*

"I can only guess that it was Bentley who carried this small, wonderful photo in his wallet."

I can only guess that it was Bentley who carried this small, wonderful photo in his wallet for a long time. It clearly shows the Santa Ana hangars and runway adjacent to the "strip." And I'm further assuming that's the Joe Nitti purple roadster making a pass with Big George at the wheel.

You've seen this photo a million times, and that's exactly why I'm showing it here. It's been copied and recopied so often, you've probably never seen young Dick Kraft's rippling muscles and deep tan. This is from the original negative. No wonder he drove without a shirt. But Krafty also told me that the beach was close enough to the track that he could bomb down there in *The Bug*, dive into the surf to cool off, and be back in time for the next round. Knowing Dick, he probably could. Whether this was truly the first "rail job" is a matter of legend.

Hot Rod Gallery   87

This photo was taken at Santa Ana on February 1, 1953, and it's a bit amazing that safety regs were still so lax: no body, no firewall, no apparent roll bar, no fear. This kid was most likely running a good dose of nitro, too.

The same day at Santa Ana, you see two more rails lined up for eliminations. At least the one in the foreground has a healthy roll bar, but no body and not much firewall. And they're wearing shirts. They might not afford much protection, but the polka-dot one is snazzy.

"This is Tony in the 1929 at Santa Ana in 1953, less hood and grille."

The Berardini Brothers fielded a pair of black roadsters that were always as fast as they were well turned out. This is Tony in the '29 at Santa Ana in 1953, less hood and grille. Soon brother Pat painted both it and his '32 with bold white flames, while Von Dutch added pinstripes and numbers. The No. 404 Deuce, named for its Isky cam, had a long and successful career as both a racer and a street rod, before being restored to its 1950s flathead, flamed form by collector Roger Morrison.

Chapter Four *The First Drag Strips*

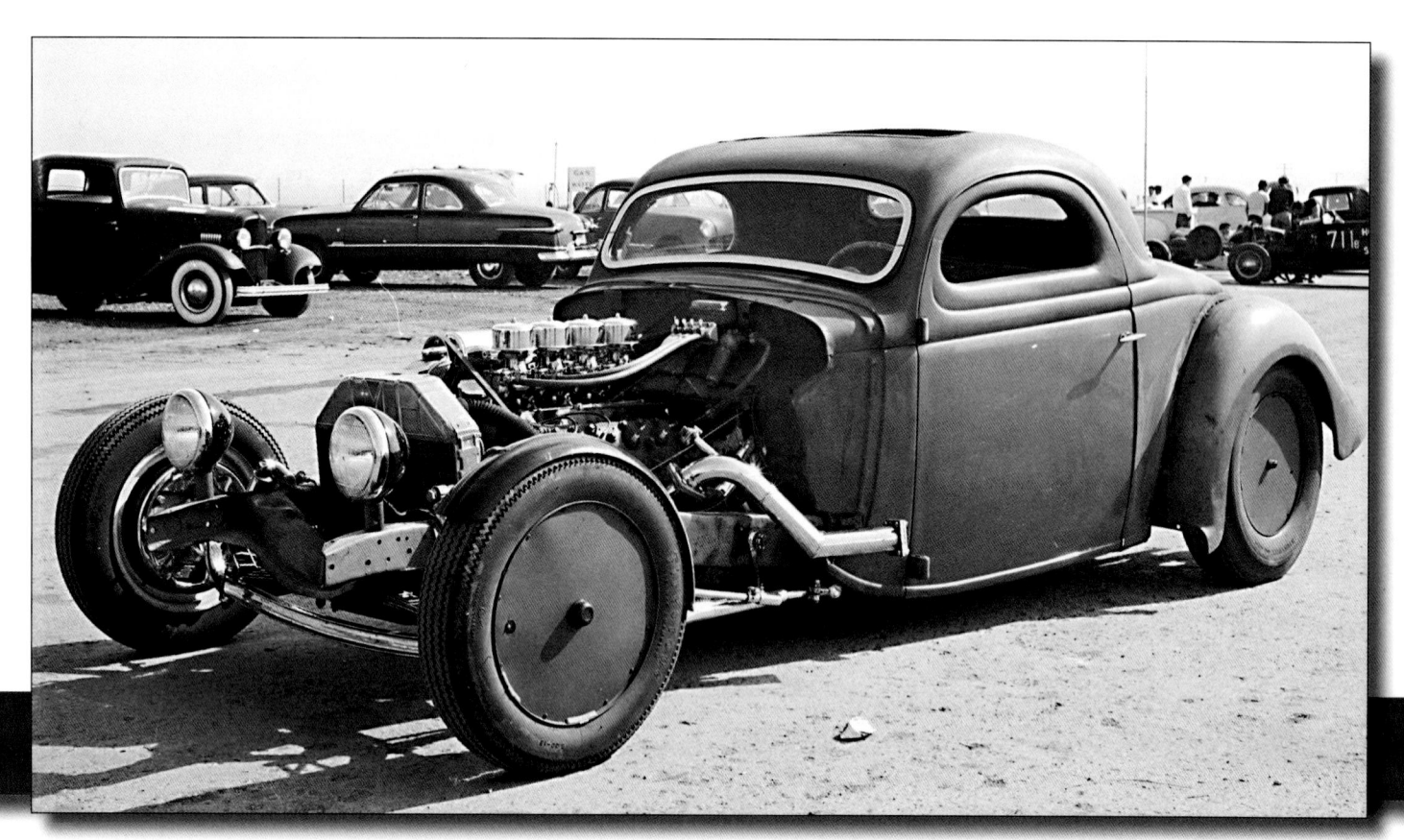

It's hard to explain the headlights on this chopped and heavily channeled 1936 coupe seen in the Santa Ana pits. In fact, it's hard to explain the completely chromed front axle, brakes, and wishbones on this otherwise unpainted car, let alone the single front cycle fender. So I won't try.

I've loved this photo for a long time: two "sits right" Deuce street roadsters lined up on what appears to be a makeshift drag strip of questionable surface, plus a timing stand with a palm-thatched roof. It could almost be a scene from an early 1950s TV sitcom, except the cars are too good and the teenage crowd too authentic. This is actually a scene from a drag meet held at the Fontana, California, airport, organized by the Choppers car club of Pomona with the help of Pomona police officer Bud Coons, using Otto Crocker's timers. A small article in the July 1951 *HRM* told how they secured insurance and FAA approval. Apparently they obtained use of the better-paved west corner of the Los Angeles County Fairgrounds shortly after this, so maybe only one or two meets were held here.

Hot Rod Gallery   89

The Six-S airport in the hills of Saugus, California, was apparently not FAA sanctioned because they had to halt weekend drags if an infrequent circling airplane wanted to land. Owned by the Bonelli family, who also owned the nearby long-running circle track, Saugus was operated from 1951 to 1954 by Lou Senter of Ansen Automotive and employee Lou Baney. You can see the portly Baney at right in this smoky photo. Senter usually stood under the tree at the far left, with a flag to stop motorists on a crossing road if a drag car overran the short shutdown.

"They had to halt weekend drags if an infrequent circling airplane wanted to land."

Saugus was popular because it was the first legal track near Los Angeles, about forty miles north, just off the road to El Mirage. As you can see in this 1953 photo, looking back down the track as two chopped 1932 coupes reach the finish line, it was just a narrow strip of asphalt, with no amenities whatsoever.

90   Chapter Four *The First Drag Strips*

This is January 11, 1953, at Saugus. You can tell it's winter because a few guys have light jackets. This track wasn't NHRA sanctioned, and safety rules seemed to be as scarce as port-a-potties, judging from these two bare-bones rail jobs. The guy in the near lane doesn't even have a helmet, and both cars are adding to liquids already spewed on the starting line.

"Both cars are adding to liquids already spewed on the starting line."

Helmets? Roll bars? Just two young kids duking it out, side-by-side on a makeshift runway drag strip in 1953. At least they're not on the city streets. The 1930 A-V-8 on Deuce rails displays So-Cal and Kong signage, but the car doesn't look familiar.

Hot Rod Gallery

The NHRA adopted "Ingenuity in Action" as its slogan, but I doubt this contraption would pass their tech inspection: Model A wheels in front, widened 1939s in back with grooved dirt tires, the engine in the front seat, driver in the rear, with a square water-pipe roll bar in between. And this is December 1952, T-shirt weather in California.

> "At least this dragster has a nominal body and firewall."

In the pits at Saugus in 1952: At least this dragster has a nominal body and firewall (if not a roll bar). Those are Smith heads on the flathead, with a Vertex mag and a 2-71 GMC blower cleverly adapted to the engine and modified to mount three 97 carburetors.

92   Chapter Four *The First Drag Strips*

The most amazing thing about this hastily chopped 1932 five-window is the large Huth Muffler Special lettering cut with a torch in the rear deck. Other lettering indicates this was a fun-loving team, though the quick-change rear looks serious. I don't know who the stout guy in white overalls is, but the Huth Brothers Muffler shop was well known to rodders. Gerry invented the hydraulic tubing bender seen in nearly every muffler shop today, and Bill developed and ran the Willow Springs Raceway complex beginning in 1962.

What I love about this photo, besides the clean 1929 roadster itself, is the impression of speed with the spinning tires and blurred background, yet the sharp focus on the car and the intent driver. I'm pretty sure this is Bob Joehnck's car, running at Saugus in early 1953 after Goleta closed.

Hot Rod Gallery   93

"Far too little credit is given to Bob Rounthwaite's *Thingie* in the history of dragster development."

Far too little credit is given to Bob Rounthwaite's *Thingie* in the history of dragster development. It might be the first with a round-tube frame. The driver's seat is well over the rear end. In addition, he certainly understood the principle of weight transfer, well before the Ramchargers and jacked-up Gassers. Initially running Tom McLaughlin's five-carb GMC six, it was noted for being very quick off the line in 1952. It's seen here at Saugus on January 11, 1953, running a four-carb Ford V-8.

I was lucky to acquire lots of good negatives from Saugus, and this is a classic. This nice, chopped 1932 three-window with a homemade quick-change came all the way from Utah to wait its turn to run. The choppers on the right look less patient. Plenty of spectators line the strip. Saugus can also claim the first night drags (during the hot summers), using a single huge searchlight pointing down the track from this position.

Chapter Four *The First Drag Strips*

I've shown photos of this car's earlier 1930s and 1940s forms, (pages 16, 21, and 47) mentioning that it would become the famed Chrisman No. 25 dragster. Well here's Art Chrisman with a somewhat tentative smile on his face, holding yet another Top Eliminator trophy at Santa Ana in the beautiful, potent, bronze car. I have used this photo to show the helmet Von Dutch lettered for him (now in the NHRA museum, as is the car). Of course, it's the twin trophy girls that make it a classic photo.

> "Here's Art Chrisman with a somewhat tentative smile on his face, holding yet another Top Eliminator trophy at Santa Ana."

Art's uncle, Jack Chrisman, was about the same age, and the two of them chopped the top on his 1929 sedan late one night. Art also built and tuned the hot, nitro-fueled flathead Merc engine, seen here boiling the skinny slicks off the line at Santa Ana in 1954. This car not only launched an illustrious driving career for Jack, but its frenetic grille insert on the front and flying eyeball on the rear pan made Von Dutch a legend. Note the hot Harley ready to run on the right and, better yet, the airplane above it coming in to land on the adjacent runway.

Here's a dramatic photo of another car that should get more credit in the annals of dragster development. The *Lakewood Muffler Special*, with its Ardun hemi-headed Merc is not only a striking design, but is also credited with the first 140-mph run. Driver Don "Cement Head" Yates might have gotten his nickname for the obvious absence of a roll bar. I have owners listed as Clark Cagle and the Yates Brothers, though I find later reference to Mickey Thompson.

Another early drag strip was Paradise Mesa in San Diego, which was basically a flattened and paved mountaintop; it was a World War II Navy practice landing field. An amateur operation run by a group of twenty clubs operating as the San Diego Timing Association from 1951 to 1957, it spawned many name racers and used Otto Crocker's clocks. This is Paul Schiefer, of racing clutch fame, smoking off in his streamlined, rear-engined, lakes and drags 1927 T.

Chapter Four *The First Drag Strips*

"This is the engine in Don Garlits' first dragster."

You'd probably never guess it, but this is the engine in Don Garlits' first dragster, with an abbreviated 1927 T body, sometime in the mid-1950s. I copied this with my camera from a framed photo he had proudly hanging on the wall of his office in Florida.

"The notorious pump house at the left of the finish line was the only obstacle."

After initial efforts at the Fontana airport, the Pomona Choppers club, with some help from Pomona Police Department officer Bud Coons, Wally Parks', and the incipient NHRA, a fresh, smooth strip of asphalt was laid in the far west end of the huge paved parking lot of the Los Angeles County fairgrounds for drag racing beginning in 1952. The notorious pump house at the left of the finish line was the only obstacle. You can see a Mercury cruising down the adjacent street on the other side of a chain-link fence (right) as this nice, full-fendered street roadster with a Road Runners SCTA plaque gets ready to make a single run in 1952.

Hot Rod Gallery 97

This was Dick Kraft's beautiful red track roadster, which gained further fame when it appeared on the *HRM* March 1962 cover as the Seiden Brothers *Highland Plating Special*. That doesn't look like Kraft driving at a large Pomona meet to benefit a local hospital in August 1953, so I'm not sure who owned the car at this point. In this photo taken near the finish line, you can see orange groves across the street, where the Brackett Field airport is now.

98   Chapter Four *The First Drag Strips*

I was quite surprised to find several photos of this beautiful, black 1929 roadster (including one of its much-chromed, four-carb flathead) in the pits at the 1953 Pomona meet. It later belonged to my friend Paul Chamberlain when he was a member of the Los Angeles Roadsters in the early 1960s. Paul said he bought it from "some guy in Highland Park who crashed it and bent the front axle." It still had no windshield when he got it, but neither of us knows who the original builder was.

The NHRA held its first large meet at the Pomona track in 1953, so of course it imposed new safety regulations. One stipulated that engines, or at least carburetors, had to be covered, so Rounthwaite devised this "hood" for his *Thingie* and decorated it appropriately.

"Rounthwaite devised this 'hood' for his *Thingie* and decorated it appropriately."

I met Roy Fjastad in the 1970s just as he was transitioning from his SPE dragster chassis company to launching the Deuce Factory, making street rods parts and the first die-stamped repro 1932 Ford frame rails. He was an original member of the famed Road Kings of Burbank club, with a very colorful racing background, and he had a scrapbook full of great photos. Here's one of my favorites that I've never had occasion to use before. I'd title it "How Dragsters were Built in the 1950s." This is Roy's home two-car garage in the Valley, circa 1955. The full-bodied, canopied, Buick-powered dragster on the left is Don Johnson's car that appeared on the *HRM* July 1958 cover. Roy was building the one on the right for himself, using a Scotty Fenn roll bar. That's a Chrysler Hemi block in the foreground.

Hot Rod Gallery 99

I didn't realize I had this photo until I searched the proofsheet with a magnifier. It's one of Roy's earlier dragsters at San Fernando, with a home-brewed front-mount 6-71 with six 97s on a Hemi. The heads are off and lying on the ground. That's Roy's uncle, with the pipe, leaning against Roy's near-new 1953 Studebaker. Don't know the guy with hands on hips. The obvious title for this one is: "OK, what do we do now?"

Tommy Ivo says Don Johnson's rail was his first dragster ride; it was also Kent Fuller's first chassis. Here you see Ivo in his own Fuller rail, with a 6-71 blower on the nailhead Buick, perhaps surprised at how far Jack Chrisman just holeshotted him off the line in the legendary *Sidewinder* dragster at Lions in 1959. How's this for a classic drag photo?

Chapter Four: The First Drag Strips

When Lions and the NHRA imposed the notorious fuel ban from 1957 through 1963, it didn't take long for the Top Gas guys to figure out that two engines went faster than one, led once again by Jack Chrisman in the Howards Cams *Twin Bears* Chevy rail. One of the wildest, most ominous-looking, and fastest was Texan Eddie Hill's running wide, canted, side-by-side, 6-71-blown Pontiac engines and four giant rear slicks to try to put all that power to the ground.

> "It didn't take long for the Top Gas guys to figure out that two engines went faster than one."

This is from Roy Fjastad's scrapbook. I can't identify the cars or even the location. Both the carbureted, canopied car in the rear and the front-blown Hemi rail in front are burning fuel, given how they're smoking the tires. What makes this photo is the intent young man in the Mooneyes T-shirt, either taking a picture or "eyeing" his team's car's performance. No, there's no guardrail. And yes, Dean Moon was a master of marketing and publicity.

Head-porter Jocko Johnson was a freethinker and amazing craftsman. One of the only successful streamlined dragsters was this one, his white and red scalloped beauty with a hand-formed aluminum body. Pushing off in turn 9 to make a run down the strip on the backstretch of the Riverside Raceway, with Jazzy Nelson at the wheel, it turned an amazing 8.35 ET at 178.21 mph on May 3, 1959, with a rear-mounted blown-fuel Hemi. Accounts vary as to whether this body was aluminum or fiberglass, and whether Nelson or Chet Herbert built the engine. No matter. Even standing still it makes a dramatic photo.

Now, as they say, for something completely different. I don't know who the photographer was, or why he turned his lens around to the crowd behind him, but he has obviously focused on the blonde with the white-rimmed dark glasses and the up-turned, starlet-like gaze. My guess is it's Lions, around 1960. It certainly is a portrait of styles and expressions.

Chapter Four *The First Drag Strips*

It's a slightly fuzzy amateur photo, but it graphically portrays a turning point in dragster development, circa 1959. This pertains to the "outlaw" tracks still running nitro (I've previously identified this as Colton, but it's probably Riverside). Archie Ary is on the far side versus Chuck Gireth, running in the 180s. The defining factor is the 6-71-blown, two-port Hilborn-injected, 392 Chrysler Hemi, running direct-drive to the M&H slicks. Also note the similar chassis/bodies, the spoke front wheels, and pre-zoomie headers. This suddenly became the standard setup for Top Fuel; the only real difference for the next decade was increasingly longer wheelbases.

With all the attention paid to Gassers lately, let alone Fuel Altereds, it seems few remember the handful of storming blown-fuel coupes, the gnarliest and most famous of which was the metallic blue Mooneyham & Sharp No. 554. It launched a long blower-building career for affable Gene Mooneyham. Surprisingly, the all-steel 1934 was found in the 1980s by Jerry Moreland, who had Roy Brizio restore it, and then Gerry Steiner tuned and drove the blown-fuel Hemi to many smoked-in full-quarter passes, just like this one from the 1950s, at early Nostalgia Drags.

This is probably the only color photo you'll see of the Adams & McEwen *Shark Car*. I think I got the transparency from Gene Adams. This is Half Moon Bay, 1961 or 1962. The car's on fuel and Tom McEwen is driving. I consider this one of the most beautiful front-engine dragsters ever, and one of the last Olds-powered examples. It didn't remain competitive for long, and Gene soon switched to Hemi power in a lighter chassis. Many stories persist about what became of this car, but all the ones I've heard are false.

Hot Rod Gallery 103

> "It's such a good action shot that Paul Chamberlain made an oil painting of it."

This 2¼-inch transparency was attached to the one of the *Shark Car*, and it's such a good action shot that Paul Chamberlain made an oil painting of it. That's Slammin' Sammy Hale at the wheel of the light, 4-71-blown small-block Chevy Champion Speed Shop fueler; it was nearly unbeatable at Half Moon Bay, its home track. The starter in the red jacket is Andy Brizio. His son Roy recreated this car in the late 1980s, and with Sammy Hale back in the seat, it won numerous Nostalgia Drag meets until Roy finally hung it on his shop wall, where it remains today.

CHAPTER FIVE

The Early Customs

I'm not going to try to explain the American custom car here. I already wrote a whole book on that subject. Nor will I try to cover all the major builders, shops, and significant cars. I have enough photos in my files to fill several books in that regard. The photos I selected for this chapter are wonderful. Not only are the cars truly beautiful, especially if you're a fan of Streamline Moderne, but the settings of most of the photographs complement them perfectly in a variety of ways. They might be posed in front of an art deco building, a theater marquee, a brick high school, or a mid-century modern house.

Perhaps they're surrounded by young guys in baggy chinos and blue suede shoes, arcane car club jackets, or sweatshirts emblazoned with weird monsters. They could even be posed with a statuesque bathing beauty of the period. These photos are great compositions (especially in black-and-white) and they capture the essence of the era that produced these sleek, sumptuous machines.

The era I'm talking about is basically 1945 to 1955. Yes, it started before the war, and customs continued into the 1960s, although they morphed into show cars, as you shall see. I surely don't need to state that custom body builders have existed virtually as long as the automobile, both in Europe and the United States. The type of custom I'm talking about here, a style that's obvious in these photos, grew out of the same movement/genre/culture that produced hot rods.

It's been often stated that there was some rivalry between the roadster boys and the cool custom cats. Today I don't believe that's true at all. I can't say for sure because, honestly, I wasn't there. My take is that the custom style that was applied to the slightly newer, "fat-fender" cars was a direct development from, and by, the same young guys who built and raced the hot rod roadsters. In fact, many custom owners of the 1940s actually had roadsters, either previously or at the same time. Likewise, nearly all custom builders, including Barris, the Ayalas, Bertolucci, Valley Custom, even Westergard, built roadsters and other types of hot rods for customers and even for themselves. You might be surprised at how many of these early customs competed at the dry lakes (Gil Ayala, for example) because they knew that the streamlining they were creating was more than simply aesthetic.

Let's start with the practical. In the early Depression years these fat-fender cars didn't exist; the first Fords with fat fenders were 1935s and 1936s. Model T and A roadsters were available and cheap; young guys could build them into fast, sporty, exciting rods. However, you have to consider three things. First, these open roadsters were fast and fun, but not all the time. If you're still in high school that's okay. For daily transportation to work and back, it's not so good.

> *"These cars had an air of mystery about them and some even looked a bit sinister."*

Consequently (second), the young kids who built the roadsters got older, got jobs (as the Depression eased in the late 1930s and early 1940s), and not only wanted more practical and comfortable daily drivers, but they could afford something better (maybe even keeping the roadster, as well).

The third point is that some girls loved getting their hair blown in fast, loud, uncomfortable roadsters, but most didn't. A shiny car with plush upholstery and a protective top was much more appealing. Moreover, roadsters offered no privacy whatsoever. They certainly didn't have back seats. Look at these photos. You get what I'm saying.

The customs I'm talking about weren't built just to impress (or seduce) the ladies. They followed that same do-it-yourself, make-it-better ethic that produced hot rods. That's why this custom era came a little later. Even when they had jobs, most of these guys couldn't afford new cars. It started in the early 1940s; with 1935 and 1936 models they could buy used and fix up. Even if some could afford new or nearly new cars, you'll note that most were Fords, Chevys, Plymouths, and maybe some of the new mid-level Mercurys, or even a Buick.

Not only did the customizers lower, chop, and channel the cars, they also stripped them of all emblems, ornaments, and badges that identified their original make. Then they added grilles, headlights, taillights, wheel covers, and other components from Cadillacs, Packards, Lincolns, and other high-end cars. A deep, rich, hand-rubbed metallic lacquer paint job, smooth DeSoto ripple bumpers, teardrop Buick or Packard skirts, removed running boards, wide whitewall tires, and possibly a rich, white padded convertible top to match the plush two-tone tuck-and-roll upholstery transformed these once-cheap, low-end cars into striking, rich-looking,

When I met and interviewed George Du Vall in 1990, he gave me photos of some cars fitted with his beautiful V-windshields. One was a dark-colored 1934 Ford with fender skirts, LaSalle headlights, and 1940 Zephyr bumpers owned by Wes Collins in 1941 or 1942. Later I found more photos of this car in an unidentified scrapbook Bill Larzelere bought in a thrift store. The above photo of that car, painted a lighter color, wearing Du Vall ripple hubcaps and a Carson top, and parked in front of what appears to be a Hollywood Hills then-new home, was in the album. It's a wonderful mid-century-modern photo, but I can't positively identify the owner, and the car has not been seen since.

---

sleek automobiles. At the same time they had an air of mystery about them. With their chopped tops, slit windows, ground-scraping stance, covered rear wheels, and lack of identification, some even looked sinister.

The point is that while they certainly cost more to build than a stripped-down T or A roadster, these very cool customs were built (often by the owners, with help from a local body shop) from second-hand or low-priced cars to look different from, and better than, the assembly-line models available in the showrooms, even the most expensive ones. Although the builders followed certain patterns and trends defined by the culture, each car was unique and personalized. That's what a custom is. Here, you can see how the style developed.

Chapter Five *The Early Customs*

This, of course, is the Southern California Plating Company delivery truck built by Du Vall and Frank Kurtis in 1935 with George's first namesake windshield, a removable padded top, and handmade grille. The car itself is magnificent, but posing it in front of this Streamline Moderne building, at this angle, makes for a wonderful photo. The Randall Motor Club was similar to today's AAA.

This has to be the first 1940 Ford ever customized, and its story is priceless. Link Paola worked as a body/paint man at a large Ford dealership in Montrose, just north of Glendale, California. He also did custom work on the side, including chopping convertibles for Carson tops. The debut of the new 1940 DeLuxe models was a big deal for Ford in September 1939. Somehow Paola, more or less as a practical joke, was able to get one of the new DeLuxe convertibles being delivered to this dealer, straight off the train. In one week's time he chopped the windshield, filled the hood and deck, removed the running boards, and repainted it in hand-rubbed cherry red lacquer. He had already arranged with Carson to make a white top to proper dimensions. Then he bolted on DeSoto bumpers, teardrop skirts, and moon-disc hubcaps with wide whitewalls, and parked it on the main street, right in front of the dealer, on the morning the new Forties officially debuted. Of course it stole the show, and he got fired. Nevertheless, he started his own custom shop across the street. It flourished through the 1940s and even advertised in early *HRM* issues as Link's Customs. A great touch to this photo are the gas prices.

Harry Westergard of Sacramento is generally regarded as the "old master" of customizing who developed the vertical grille, sunken bullet headlghts, filled hood, teardrop skirts, ripple bumpers, teardrop spotlights, and often padded lift-off chopped-top look that became the standard in the 1940s. This is an early version of his work on a 1939 Ford owned in 1946 by Mel Falconer. Later Westergard made a steel removable top for it and shaved the handles, using (possibly the first) push-button solenoids to open the doors.

Convertible sedans were popular for early customs. Although Westergard more often than not used Packard grilles, for Norm Milne's 1938 Ford he installed the tall Cadillac LaSalle frequently credited to him. In this good photo that Norm took and sent me, it's seen with its filled hood still in primer in front of his gas station, with Gene Garrett's chopped 1940 convertible in the background. The guys who hung out here were into rods and customs, and became the nucleus of the Sacramento Thunderbolts car club, which is still active. Milne had a good camera, and sent me several good negatives from this era.

Chapter Five *The Early Customs*

I saw this photo hanging on the wall in Joe Bailon's den, and was quite surprised when he told me, "That's Tommy The Greek's, and it's the first custom I saw, in Richmond, in 1941." From what I understand Tommy did his own body and paint, but went to Carson in Los Angeles to get the tan top done. With a shaved and filled hood, deck, and running boards, teardrop skirts, later bumpers, and ripple disk caps, it certainly had that custom look, even then. The way he has his Appleton spotlights turned was apparently the Bay Area style at that time.

"It has an incredible history including trips across the country, up the capitol steps, and through jungles of South America."

You've very likely seen these great photos before, but I'm including them because (1) Doane Spencer pulled these 8 x 10 prints out of his very messy desk drawer, (2) very few color photos from this era exist, and (3) Jimmy Summers, whose shop was in Hollywood, was not only the first well-known "customizer" in the area, but this is his own 1940 Mercury that he chopped and channeled with a sectioned hood and raised fenders, plus a Buick-inspired handmade grille. It had a seldom-used Carson top. In addition, it has an incredible history including trips across the country, up the capitol steps, and through jungles of South America. Yes, it still exists.

A difficult but popular custom trick in the 1940s was called "full fadeaways," where the front fenderline was extended down through the door and rear quarter to the back fender, in streamlined fashion similar to 1942–1948 Buicks. Jimmy Summers made a bolt-on kit to do this on Chevys, and I assume Westergard used it, molding them to the body, when building this near-new 1946 convertible for Butler Rugard (in the cuffed Levis). Its chopped and padded top came from Hall's in Oakland. Customs generally used grilles from Packards, Cadillacs, and other pricey cars; but the lower horizontal 1946 Lincoln unit seen here (and on others) didn't work well.

> "I ran the pictures in *R&C*, and the readers loved the car, but had no clues to its whereabouts. It's gorgeous, but gone. Why not duplicate it?"

The Bistagne Brothers Body Shop is still the best in the Glendale area, just blocks from my house. Several years ago, recently departed brother George brought me these two slightly fuzzy photos of this classic 1938 Ford DeLuxe convertible sedan that he customized when it was one year old, and asked if I could locate it. I ran the pictures in *R&C*, and the readers loved the car, but had no clues to its whereabouts. Painted metallic Ruby Maroon, special features included filled hood sides, formed covers where running boards were removed, rear fender gravel shields, a nicely recessed rear license, and the use of 1934 Cabriolet windows in the rear doors to give the chopped Carson top a rounded edge. It's gorgeous, but gone. Why not duplicate it?

110 Chapter Five *The Early Customs*

Burbank is right next to Glendale, and Neil Emory was a high school student there in 1940–1941 when he built this unusual 1937 Dodge into a surprisingly good-looking custom. A body shop chopped the windshield (for a Carson top) and painted it gloss black, but young Neil shaved it, added 1939 Ford taillights, and recessed two plates in the rear (license and club plaque) in shop class. Obviously the kid had talent. He and brother-in-law Clay Jensen opened Valley Custom after the war, where they did exquisite work.

Here's another perfect mid-century custom. Art Lellis' dark green chopped, channeled, and semi-sectioned 1939 convertible usually sat next to partner Jerry Moffat's similar gold one in front of their Olive Hill Garage in Hollywood to attract customers. They were mechanics, but did all their own custom work. Dale Runyan did the upholstery and the padded tops, adding a "panoramic" three-piece rear window to this one. Also note the rumble seat lid, small motorcycle taillights, and chrome fender welt. Among few customs featured in early *HRMs*, both appeared on the last page of the September 1948 issue.

Hot Rod Gallery 111

"I show this photo because it's a cool car, and also because the photo of George's Buick is so similar."

This photo was among a great stash loaned to me by Hershel "Junior" Conway. It's a 1947 Cadillac. It's heavily chopped with a Carson top. And I assume it's in front of the Barris Brothers first shop on Compton Avenue in South Los Angeles, where they were doing further custom work on this near-new, high-end car. I show it because it's a cool car, and also because the photo of George's Buick (below) is so similar.

"What I love about the rear shot is the near-identical convertible, with fadeway fenders, in a similar stage of construction across the street."

The first finished custom that made a name for George Barris was this chopped, Carson-topped 1941 Buick convertible to which he added full fadeaway fenders and a cut-down 1941 Cadillac grille. It was reportedly the only custom in the January 1948 SCTA Hot Rod Exposition, and it made the cover of the May 1948 *Road & Track*. I thought these were early construction photos, but on second look you notice the grille is a cut-down 1947 Cadillac version. George had wrecked the car, and was redoing it at the Compton Avenue shop (which he said he left in late 1949). The bumpers with the lights in the guards are 1946–1947 Olds. What I love about the rear shot is the near-identical convertible, with fadeway fenders, in a similar stage of construction across the street.

112   Chapter Five *The Early Customs*

Bill Faris' 1938 Ford was chopped maybe even a bit more than Neal Emory's, and they were members of the same car club, so perhaps Neal did this one while he was still in high school, or shortly after. Have you noticed how each early custom shown so far is different, yet they have a certain similar look? Further, all have chopped, non-folding, padded tops. That's because cutting and welding a flat-glass windshield was simple, and you could let the upholsterer make the top to fit. Unlike earlier hot rods, chopping the rounded steel tops of 1936–1948 coupes took considerably more metalworking skill.

When Neal Emory and Clay Jensen opened Valley Custom in Burbank in 1948, one of their first efforts was Ray Vega's 1938 convertible sedan, which they did in the early Carson-top style. Unlike Bistagne's, however, they channeled the body, retained the running boards, and swapped on a 1940 DeLuxe front end with the fenders raised and the hood sectioned, filled, and peaked to fit. It also got newer bumpers and 1941 Studebaker taillights. I love the photo below, taken in Griffith Park with the road winding off in the distance.

You saw a front shot of Jesse Lopez' green 1941 Ford with a cut-down 1947 Cadillac grille in Chapter Three on page 74. This rear angle, taken at another outdoor car show, demonstrates not only a very skillful, smoothly sloping chop by Sam and George Barris on this steel, "turret-top" coupe, but also a slightly new style. It still has the skirted, tail-dragging stance, but note the fenders molded to the body, shaved driprails and door handles, custom taillights inset in the bumper guards, and the new 1949 Cadillac "sombrero" wheel covers.

Meanwhile, another pair of brothers, Gil and Al Ayala, were doing surprisingly similar custom work at their shop in East Los Angeles. Gil seemed to like the 1942 Ford grille, and this is his own severely (but smoothly) chopped 1942 coupe appropriately posed in front of Garfield High. Reportedly painted dark gold, smooth is the operative word for this whole car. Note the large radius, formed with welded-in sheet metal, between the rear fender and body, as well as the frenched headlights, molded-in taillight pods, and completely shaved body.

114 Chapter Five *The Early Customs*

In the San Francisco East Bay area, Joe Bailon represented the second generation of customizers and launched his long, significant, and highly stylized career with *Miss Elegance,* his completely customized 1941 Chevy coupe, seen here at the third Oakland show in 1952. His hand-formed tube grilles and scoops with chrome teeth became hallmarks. An extra I love about this particular photo is the glimpse of the chopped 1947 Chevy convertible with the "mail-slot" rear window behind it.

> "Whereas customs of the era were regarded as heavy, slow 'leadsleds,' John told me this was his street-racing 'sleeper.'"

John Geraghty had a long and illustrious career building hot rods and high-horsepower engines, so it may come as a surprise that the Ayalas built this chopped, channeled, and cleanly shaved 1940 convertible for him. You might note the hood is slightly sectioned, the running boards are molded off, and it has no skirts, spotlights, handles, or any extras. Nor does it drag on the ground. Whereas customs of the era were regarded as heavy, slow "leadsleds," John told me this was his street-racing "sleeper." Built in the late 1940s, it sat on a lightweight custom tube chassis and had a very potent flathead under the hood.

Hot Rod Gallery   115

Although it's still a Carson-topped, fat-fender convertible, the 1939 Mercury that Valley Custom built for Glen Hooker, their sixteen-year-old brother-in-law, looks thinner and more modern. Valley's trick (their specialty) was cutting a horizontal section out of these fat 1940s or slab-sided 1950s cars to literally thin them. They also left the skirts off, made it sit more level (though still lowered), and then cut the wheelwells higher, giving their customs a sportier, newer look. On this one, they cheated by channeling the body over the frame and then trimming off the bottom of the body and fenders. I like this photo with the "modern art" in the background.

I include this picture largely because it's a complete mystery to me. I figure it's in San Francisco and probably a 1941 Chevy (or Olds). I showed it to Joe Bailon, thinking it had his "look," but he had no clue. Note the spotlights turned the same way as Tommy the Greek's. The chop, bodywork, and paint look nice. Even the bumpers are shaved. The hand-formed grille is its striking element. I did spot it in a "Grille Ideas" feature in an early *HRM*, showing this and a later revision, but no identification of the car or builder.

116 Chapter Five *The Early Customs*

I had to show this photo, even though by now it's a classic. This original Nick Matranga 1940 Merc has been copied and cloned more often than any other car I know. Not only did Sam and George Barris use pieces formed by California Metal Shaping to smoothly blend the rear roof into the trunkline, but they also cut the windshield less than the top to make it less "squinty." They removed the B-pillar to make it a hardtop (the latest thing in 1950–1951 new cars) and created the striking curved chrome frames where the side and quarter windows meet. George called the color Royal Maroon with Gold Iridescent. I also wanted to show this profile shot at South-Central's Fremont High to complement Gil Ayala's car at East Los Angeles' Garfield High on page 113.

The introduction of the new, longer, lower Mercury in 1949 marked a new genre in customizing in the early 1950s. The 1949–1951 Mercs were to customs what the 1955–1957 Chevys were to hot rodding. It's often been stated that the new Mercury retained enough of the old lines (fat, rounded body; vestigial fenders; flat-paned V-windshield) that customizers knew immediately what to do to it. Yet it's uncanny how Sam Barris and the Ayalas both cut into new 1949s almost identically. (I assume you know Sam's green 1949.) The Ayalas were building this one for Louie Bettancourt at the same time, and the first thing both did was hammer the "hump" out of the door to give a full fadeaway fenderline. The only real difference was that the Ayalas slanted the B-pillar and rounded the hood corners. This is a later photo, after Barris painted Louie's car deep maroon, made a new grille, and added bumper guards. It's my favorite Merc, and I chose this photo for the 1950s theater in the background.

Hot Rod Gallery 117

"This one is both beautiful and snarky at the same time . . . exactly the idea."

I have few photos of Sam Barris; he's in the same grubby clothes in most of them because he was always working. Junior Conway took this color picture, with his "Sam Bronze" 1950 Ford just finished in its first form, including some minimal Von Dutch striping. That's Sam's blue family 1952 Ford convertible in the background.

I include this photo for three simple reasons: First, I have it. Second, of the original radical Mercs built in the 1950s, this is by far the most seldom seen, and has long since disappeared. Third, it was the second 1949 Merc Sam chopped (for Jerry Quesnel); he went even further, chopping it lower than any other he did. With its slanted B-pillar, rounded and peaked hood, frenched lights, simple grille, deep purple paint, and very low stance, this one is both beautiful and snarky at the same time . . . exactly the idea.

You might notice I'm not including a photo of the Bob Hirohata Merc, even though I have dozens. You've seen 'em. I'm pretty sure you've never seen this shot of Jesse Lopez' Ford. From Junior Conway's stash, he simply had "Drag Meet?" penciled on the back. Note the guy writing a number in the quarter window. Check out these dudes and their threads. You couldn't have posed this if you tried. I like the one in the polka-dot shirt on the left. And what about the guy on the right with the Dingfods club jacket?

Chapter Five *The Early Customs*

I wish the sign weren't leaning against it, and I wish the photo were in color. Buster Litton's 1949 Ford is, in my opinion, the most nicely customized of all shoebox Fords. Done between 1951 and 1953 with mostly new parts, the beautifully proportioned hardtop roof chop was performed at Barris' shop. Then it went to nearby George Cerny's, where he smoothly grafted on 1951 Olds 98 rear fenders and 1951 Studebaker fronts/headlights next to a peaked and lipped hood. He finished it off with 1953 Chevy grille pieces, new 1953 Cadillac wheel covers, and Cocoa Rust lacquer, which looked more like cinnamon.

Although customizing was even more trend-driven than hot rodding, there were some who held to the old school, even in the early days. Actually it was only five years after Bob Pierson's white, skirted 1936 coupe appeared on the August 1948 cover of *HRM* that Jim McKinley's clean, chopped, quite similar example was featured inside (October 1953). However, in rod or custom years, that's decades. Often confused, with its ripple bumpers, lowered headlights, solid (but louvered) hood, and small hubcaps, the main difference was molded running boards with MG rub strips on McKinley's, who was a local custom upholsterer. The grille and wheels were bright red.

Junior had this wonderful photo, but he couldn't remember who took it or why, possibly for a local newspaper. The studly guy was his friend Don Ferrar, who "built the whole car in his backyard . . . had a roadster, too." You can see that he's already done some nice leadwork on the car, such as the filled hood, frenched lights, molded custom grille, and flared front fenders. But since it's finished in a coat of white primer with fresh chrome, I hope he's not planning to do anything with that lit torch, grinder, or lead files . . . other than get his photo taken.

The guy with the coat, cigarette, and pencil moustache is Harold "Baggy" Bagdasarian, so this must be the Sacramento Autorama, which he promoted from the beginning (later acquiring the Oakland Roadster Show as well). Of course that's a smiling young George Barris on the left, and the flamed fender belongs to Jim Griepsma's yellow 1934 coupe, which he had just gotten on the *Life of Riley* TV show and, subsequently, on the December 1956 *HRM* cover with William Bendix. Title this one "Two Promoters."

120   Chapter Five *The Early Customs*

While some readers hopefully appreciated tanned, shirtless Don Ferrar, I must say that this unfortunately unnamed young lady posing with Junior's bronze Ford is the prettiest swimsuit model I've seen. Again, that's personal opinion, of course. Junior doesn't remember anything about it. "It was something George cooked up. I was probably in the back, working."

"Rather than shaving, cleaning, and streamlining, this is the beginning of the 'more is better' phase."

Hot Rod Gallery   121

Gratuitous cheesecake? Well, George was promoting something. And she is pretty. But what I'm really showing here is a glimpse of Barris' new shop truck, *Kopper Kart,* which perfectly illustrates the next phase in custom trends, largely engendered by the new car shows. Rather than shaving, cleaning, and streamlining, this is the beginning of the "more is better" phase. Besides a chopped top, you can see lots of chrome (and Kopper), multiple pipes, plenty of scallops and pinstriping, tons of tuck-and-roll, and an upholstered top. She's talking on the phone and, yes, that is a TV on the bed.

The *R&C* magazine "Dream Truck" evolved over several years of supposed readers suggestions for modifications. In fact this was a case of editor/owner Spence Murray involving many name customizers of the time, each adding their own modifications to the project that continued, and morphed, from 1954 to 1958. Shown here in its best-known white pearl and purple scalloped form, it turned out looking more like a svelte horse than a committee-built camel.

Chapter Five *The Early Customs*

I could have included this photo in Chapter Six on shops, but it exemplifies another new trend in customizing in the latter 1950s. This 1957 Chevy is brand new, straight from the dealer. The new 1957–1960 hardtops came from the factory with lowered roofs, sweeping tailfins, dual headlights, and scoops—styling essentially aped from earlier customs. Kids out of high school with a job could buy one on time, drive it to the muffler shop to have it lowered and some pipes installed, maybe change the hubcaps, then make an appointment at The Crazy Painters, where Baron, Roth & Kelly could mask it, scallop it, and pinstripe it in a matter of hours, and you had an instant custom.

Although Von Dutch really started it, the wild, crazy painting and its ancillary, the "Weirdo" airbrushed sweatshirt, became the latest fad fueled by the work of Dean Jeffries, Ed "Big Daddy" Roth, and Larry Watson. Roth assumed a Beatnik persona, and that's one way to describe these car club guys wearing some early versions of his airbrushed artwork. By 1957–1958, these were the guys you hoped didn't beat you up after school, or steal the hubcaps off your car. Check the horseshoe taps on the shoes of the guy on the right.

Hot Rod Gallery   123

Young Tom Kelly took these photos with his Brownie, so they're a little fuzzy. This 1949 Chevy fastback, although not brand-new, is still a perfect example. The only bodywork was shaving the hood and trunk. Otherwise it's lowered on a rake, with side pipes, flipper caps, dummy spots, and a whole lot of crazy scallops to make it a plenty wild standout in 1957 traffic.

"Here's just one tribute to the recently departed Dean Jeffries, who painted the way Tina Turner sang: all-out and to the max."

Here's just one tribute to the recently departed Dean Jeffries, who painted the way Tina Turner sang: all-out and to the max. Smiley Polk's near-stock black 1950 Ford sedan probably got nosed and decked at Barris' shop, since it has a Kustoms Los Angeles plaque in the back window. In 1957, Jeffries (whose small shop was next door) set it afire with a whole lot of white and red-tipped "curly flames." Dean was never known for subtlety.

124 Chapter Five *The Early Customs*

The thing about Joe Bailon's prolific customs of the 1950s is that you either love them or you don't. I love Richard Del Curto's finned 1950 Ford coupe from 1958, painted by Joe in his signature candy apple red lacquer over base-gold accents.

Hot Rod Gallery   125

By 1959, when Dee Wescott built this 1936 Ford roadster with a LaSalle grille, lowered headlights, and ripple bumpers for Bob Hooper of Beaverton, Oregon, it was completely out of style, especially with its full-moon wheel covers. The only concessions to the times were side pipes, white running boards, and medium white sidewalls. Spence Murray built one much like this in the early 1970s, which helped spark the reacceptance of earlier rod and custom styles, which are fully appreciated today. So much the better.

"Pow! This photo hits you right between the eyes, doesn't it? That's exactly what Bailon intended."

Pow! This photo hits you right between the eyes, doesn't it? That's exactly what Bailon intended. Actually, it was his customer, Frank Caraway, who bought the 1958 Impala new, drove it straight to Bailon's shop, and said, "Make it really wild." Joe added thirty scoops in the body and painted it pink. After one show season, Caraway brought it back and said, "Make it wilder. I really want to win big." So Joe did, as you can see here.

"The thing about Joe Bailon's prolific customs of the 1950s is that you either love them or you don't."

CHAPTER SIX

Early Hot Rod Shops and Speed Parts

One of the first stories I did for The Rodder's Journal, in issue No. 4, was called "The Grand Shop Tour." I say I "did" it, rather than "wrote" it, because this was more of a performance piece than a literary piece. The premise was that most of the first speed shops, parts manufacturers, custom builders, etc. began around the Los Angeles/Orange County area just before and after World War II. Of course I was born during that period and wasn't old enough to visit any of those shops then. However, along with collecting photographs over the past forty years, I have also been collecting early hot rod and custom car magazines, along with SCTA and other dry lakes racing programs and newsletters going back to the 1930s. Most of these early hot rod businesses had small ads in them. The ads had addresses. Nearly all of those addresses were within driving distance of my house. So . . .

I'm sure it started when I first subscribed to *Hot Rod* and also bought the little magazines off the rack at the grocery store. The ads always intrigued me, and I'd try to visualize where these places were, and what they looked like, especially inside where the parts were made. There's more to tell, but I did in that article, so I'll keep it brief here.

Actually, finding those early speed shops was akin to searching out lost hot rods. It's another element of hot rod archeology, which, as you know, is one of my favorite subjects.

My first actual hunt happened when I moved to Glendale about twenty-five years ago. I had been building (and breaking) inline Chevy sixes in my '48 since high school, and therefore had a particular interest in Chevy and GMC six hop-up parts. In fact, while in college in Los Angeles, I learned that the McGurk Equipment Company had merged with Iskenderian Cams. I went down to the big Isky factory on Broadway in South Los Angeles (the first time I'd seen it or been there) to buy a steel billet McGurk cam, complete with chilled iron solid lifters and tubular pushrods, to install in my Chevy six.

"In fact, at this point I'm already feeling as if I'm trying to stuff way too much into this fifty-pound bag."

When I got to Glendale, I remembered that the Wayne Horning Manufacturing Company, makers of the renowned twelve-port cylinder heads for Chevy and GMC sixes, was located on Fletcher Drive in Glendale. As I said in the 1995 article, "one of the first things I did was look up the address of Wayne Manufacturing, find it on the map, and drive down to see what was there. Standing there looking at the small, square, unassuming building at 3206 Fletcher and realizing that this was where the famous twelve-port heads for GMC and Chevy sixes were made gave me a certain sense of discovery and excitement. Little did I know that later I would own not one, but two of those heads."

In fact, I quickly discovered that "the vast majority of those first hot rod emporiums were located in Los Angeles proper, or in neighboring cities. In fact, a surprising number of them were located right here in Glendale: Ed Winfield, Kurtis Kraft, Barney Navarro, Weiand, A. J. Watson, Wayne Manufacturing, Venolia Pistons, Stelling gearboxes, not to mention the first offices of *Hop Up*, *Rod & Custom*, and *Road & Track* magazines."

I have no idea how many sites I found, visited, and photographed while doing that story. Way more than would fit in the magazine. But that's when I met and became friends with people such as Barney Navarro and Kong Jackson; Spence Murray showed me the first *R&C* office, the Link Paola custom shop where he once worked, and the site of Valley Custom. It's exciting just remembering all that.

Of course, I also scrounged early photos of many of these places. That was the impetus for this chapter,

I have absolutely no idea where I got this photo, where it was taken, nor exactly when. But it's a wonderful photo, isn't it? You undoubtedly know that the Gilmore Oil Company not only was a major sponsor of auto racing, and of specific cars, but also built one of the bigger, better racetracks in Los Angeles, the Gilmore Stadium (later home of the PCL Los Angeles Angels, now the site of CBS TV City). Judging by the prices, I'd guess this is late 1920s or early 1930s. In addition, you might think Shady Grove Service is out in the boonies; but check that divided, paved, two-lane street it's on. This type of road in sprawling SoCal nearly invited roadster racing.

---

but there's no way I could include all that here. In fact, at this point I'm already feeling as if I'm trying to stuff way too much into this fifty-pound bag. It's the usual problem. There's just too much good stuff. What you have instead is a potpourri of places, pieces, speed parts, and complete engines that I've pulled out of my files because I think you'll find them interesting, surprising, and in a few cases, mystifying. See what you think.

Chapter Six *Early Hot Rod Shops and Speed Parts*

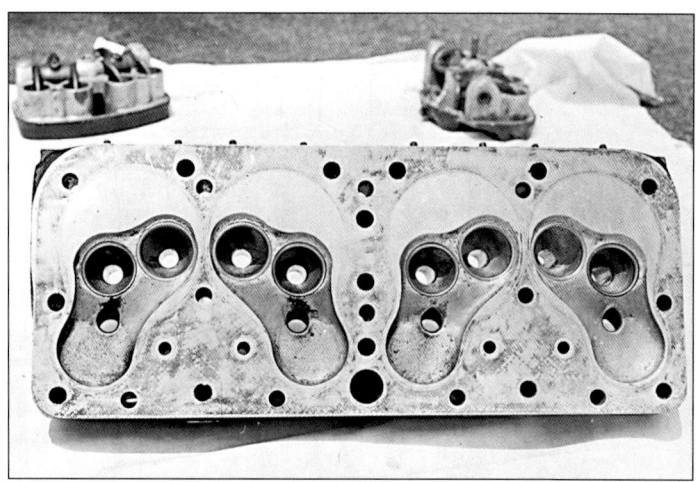

In terms of engines and hot rod parts, let's start with Ford four-bangers because that's where rodding really started, with speed shops such as Bell Auto Parts (in Bell, California) selling used race car parts. George Riley, who opened a large factory in East Los Angeles as early as 1922, designed and built many parts for these engines, beginning with cylinder heads and carburetors for Model Ts, progressing to his best-known two- and four-port cylinder heads for Model B Fords in the mid-1930s, to OHV conversion heads for Ford V-8s, and to complete SOHC racing V-8 engines. This is a good look at a Riley four-port, installed on an engine with a pair of Riley side-draft carbs, and looking at its combustion chambers. Affording 10:1 to 14:1 compression, this F-head had two overhead intake valves per cylinder, but retained the in-block exhaust valves and ports. In the bare head photo, you see the rocker arm assemblies in the background. Besides circle trackers, many early lakes racers ran Riley four-ports to surprising speeds.

One reason I love this photo is because Dick Bertolucci took it on his honeymoon trip to Los Angeles in 1948, when he stopped to visit his pals George and Sam Barris at their shop at 7674 Compton Avenue. This is Sam's own, dark metallic green 1940 Merc convertible with a Carson top, parked beside the shop on 76th Place. Like so many of Sam's cars, he didn't own it long, selling it to raise cash. Not only was the building still there in 1995, so was the sign on the pole behind the Merc.

Hot Rod Gallery   129

"This is my favorite custom car, especially from this angle."

Dick Bertolucci has owned a large, thriving bodyshop business in Sacramento for decades, but this is where he started. It's some time before 1948, he's eighteen years old, and he had already hand-formed the gorgeous steel lift-off top for Buddy Ohanesian's 1940 Mercury convertible sedan, as well as painted it Ruby Maroon. In the larger photo you notice add-on taillights and a trailer hitch (this was Buddy's daily driver, which towed his race car). The smaller photo is slightly later; it shows the 1946 taillights on pods molded to the rear fenders, and exhaust tips through the bumper. This is my favorite custom car, especially from this angle.

Chapter Six Early Hot Rod Shops and Speed Parts

You saw the back of Dan Busby's beautiful black 1927 T roadster at the first SCTA Hot Rod Exposition in Chapter Three on page 63, where it was wearing a boat-type V-windshield. These photos must be earlier than that, and the scene is the Anaheim backyard shop of one of the most overlooked hot rod craftsmen of the 1940s and 1950s, Marvin Webb. That's Marv's own V-windshield roadster on the right, which competed at the first Bonneville in 1949 and won the first Indy car show. I assume that's Busby in the T, recently painted in the small garage at the left rear. I also assume Webb hand-formed the nose, hood, and belly pans on this car, as he did on several others, including a couple of Dick Kraft's. The newer tin building on the right is where Marv's son Dennis does amazing metalwork today, learned from his dad and his friend Art Engels. Someday I'll tell the story of the whole Orange County hot rod gang. Thank goodness Marvin Webb had several vintage photos he shared with me years ago.

"Ever seen or even heard of an Alexander OHV V-8?"

Ever seen or even heard of an Alexander OHV V-8? This beautiful, chromed version was on display in a rolling Deuce chassis at the first SCTA Hot Rod Exposition. Apparently these were F-heads made for 21-stud Ford V-8s, with overhead exhaust valves feeding into two siamesed round ports per side. It looks like it accepts a stock intake manifold, and the spark plugs appear to be on the intake side. I know Speedy Bill Smith has one of these in his Speedway Motors museum (possibly this one?), and I've seen one other in a 1934 coupe. But that's all I've been able to find out.

Hot Rod Gallery   131

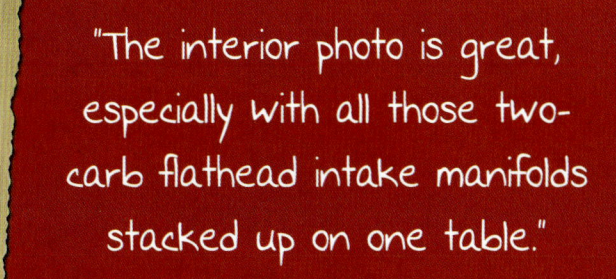

"The interior photo is great, especially with all those two-carb flathead intake manifolds stacked up on one table."

I used the exterior photo of this early Offenhauser factory on National Boulevard in West Los Angeles in 1946 or 1947 in my "Shop Tour" story. Those are founders Fred Offenhauser (nephew of the Indy engine maker, without an apron) and Fran Hernandez (on the far right). And the building was still there. This previously unseen interior photo is great, especially with all those two-carb flathead intake manifolds stacked up on one table.

Chapter Six: *Early Hot Rod Shops and Speed Parts*

> "It was the perfect low-budget engine to power midget race cars that became very popular in the postwar years."

Henry Ford wasn't about to make a six-cylinder for customers who wanted an economy engine after he introduced the revolutionary, affordable V-8 in 1932. So from 1937 to 1940 he made this pint-size flathead V-8, called the V-8-60 (rated at 60 hp). It was the perfect low-budget engine to power midget race cars that became so popular in the postwar years. Consequently most of the hop-up companies made go-fast parts for it. This one sports Evans finned heads and two-carb intake, an Eddie Meyer finned front cover mounting a Harmon-Collins mag, and nice W headers possibly by Belond. Actually, given the direction of the water inlet/outlets, this one might have been for a small hydroplane.

Even the Beach Boys knew a hot flathead had to be "ported and relieved," but not many knew what that actually meant. In this great demonstration photo, you can see that the intake ports have not only been ground slightly larger, but also shiny-smooth. This is known as being "ported and polished." More pertinent, and exclusive, to flatheads is "relieving." That is, grinding the area in the block surface between the valves and the cylinder into a shallow trough to give a slightly smoother, larger passage for both intake and exhaust charges, as is being done here.

Hot Rod Gallery   133

The Eddie Miller rear-engine streamlined lakester, literally backyard-built (note hedge behind car) in 1946–1950, was a masterpiece of engineering, fabrication, and metalwork, including numerous one-off cast-aluminum components. Thankfully it was preserved by the Ferguson family and finally exquisitely restored. But one thing has never been fully explained: why they (Eddie Sr. and Jr.) chose a Pontiac flathead six for power, other than "it was different," or "nobody wanted them, so they were cheap." In this mid-construction photo, you might notice the engine is tilted slightly, four Zenith side-drafts have been adapted (with fuel lines partly run), and one exhaust header has been crafted. The Millers also cast their own finned-aluminum head and other parts. It took forever to finish, and only ran a few times. Bill Burke once told me Eddie Sr. didn't want Eddie Jr. to go fast in it, especially after they saw and repaired Stu Hilborn's mangled car. I think it was a classic case of building it being more important than driving it.

> "I think it was a classic case of building it being more important than driving it."

Several engine/parts photos like this were black-and-white "positives," or slides, stored in a special metal filing box. I think Bill Burke used them during sales presentations when he was Ad Manager at *HRM* in its first years; these were the latest in aftermarket speed components. After partners Wayne Horning and Harry Warner split up, this new design by Wayne, with evenly spaced intake and exhaust valves, became the Horning twelve-port GMC head.

134 Chapter Six *Early Hot Rod Shops and Speed Parts*

I could write a whole story about this one photo and I could easily write a whole book about Chet Herbert. That's young Chet in his wheelchair sitting behind his Horning twelve-port GMC in his chopped and channeled 1932 four-door sedan. Not only did this car run an auto trans and hand controls, but it was powered by propane (or nitro), and was featured in *HRM*, complete with a cutaway drawing. Herbert pioneered roller cams, built fast streamliners and dragsters, and appeared on *HRM* covers. This car next appeared with a flathead V-8 and Von Dutch striping, then disappeared.

Hot Rod Gallery   135

"If Eddie Miller had chosen a Ford flathead six, he wouldn't have had to make so many of his own parts."

If Eddie Miller had chosen a Ford flathead six, he wouldn't have had to make so many of his own parts. Another camshaft wizard, Clay Smith, is credited for figuring out how to make it rev and run. I can't see a name on the finned-aluminum head or nice cast exhaust headers on this one, but the three-carb intake says "Knudsen Downey Cal." And the side cover says "Wilson."

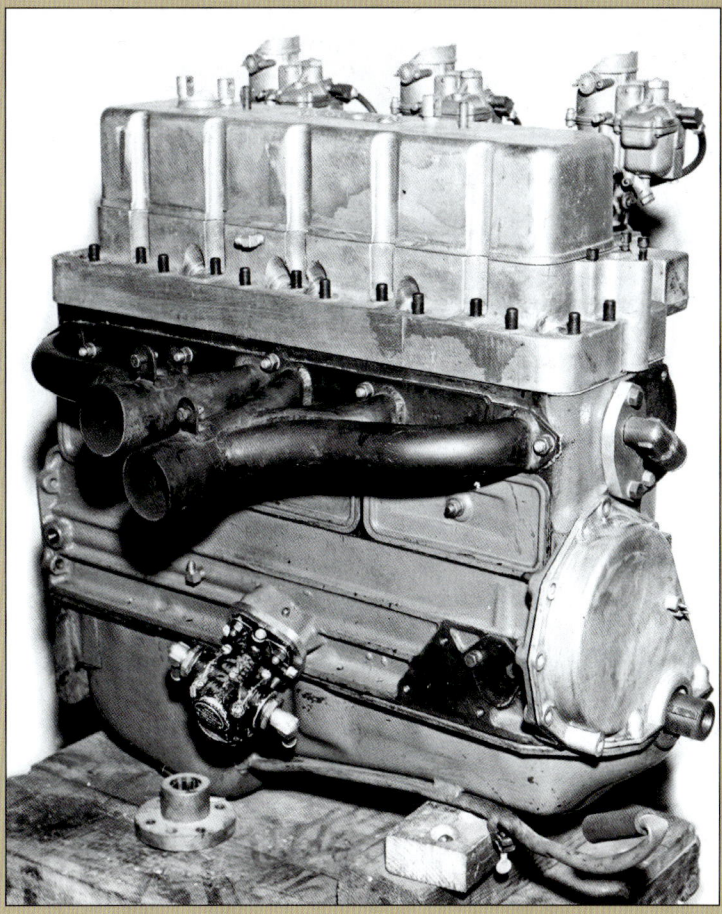

Even with the external oil pump and three tappet covers, I can't identify this flathead six engine, let alone the substantial F-head on top, fitted with a three-carb intake manifold. Given the used look of the headers, modified pan, etc., I'd guess the engine was raced as a flathead, and this head (note it's not bolted down) is a fresh prototype. It looks like a nice piece. I've never seen one on a running engine; have you?

At first I thought this was another mystery F-head. But on close inspection, I can see this is the intake side of the one above seen on the engine, with the valve cover off to show nicely cast rocker arms and pedestals. The siamesed ports indicate this was pre-Hilborn injection era. I see no name on this casting, anywhere.

Chapter Six *Early Hot Rod Shops and Speed Parts*

J.E.M. is cast in the intake manifold under the pruned 4-71 GMC blower on this 1949–1950 Cadillac. I know this company also made similar manifolds and multi-V-belt drives for small GMCs on flatheads at this time, as well. The polished cast-aluminum elbow mounting a Zephyr side-draft carb appears to be part of the well-made kit. The company didn't last, and few were made.

> "J.E.M. is cast in the intake manifold under the pruned 4-71 GMC blower on this 1949-1950 Cadillac."

This good color photo of the front of the Barris shop on Atlantic Boulevard is significant for a couple of reasons. First, it spells Kustom with a K. Second, it was painted by Von Dutch. He even signed it in the lower right corner. The long "tail" in the E in Office is pure Dutch. And wouldn't you know he'd spell it "Barri's"? The brick wall on the right is the building that housed Dean Jeffries' small shop.

And here's a rare glimpse inside Dean Jeffries' shop (note the brick wall) sometime in the mid-1950s. I got the photo from Junior Conway, and I don't think it's ever been shown before. In fact the original shot showed more, but I cropped in so you could study the details of the stuff in there. Of course that's Dean's girlfriend Carol, who had the new flamed 1956 Chevy that you have seen many times. There's a good chance Dean took the photo himself.

Chapter Six: Early Hot Rod Shops and Speed Parts

Besides Tony Nancy's shop, Bill Colgan's was the place to go for custom upholstery in the Valley in the 1950s. Bob Hoshiko was a stitcher who worked there for years, and who had several nice rods and customs. That's his bronze 1947 Mercury with molded taillights and other work by Valley Custom. He took this color photo of it posed in front of the tiny pink building. I don't know when Colgan's closed, but that same tiny building is still right there today on Hollywood Way, just north of Magnolia, in Burbank.

In Downey, the place to get your hot rod or race car upholstered was Don's Trim Shop. In fact, with a good parts store on one side, and a hot rod–friendly garage on the other, it was a good place for rodders to hang out. So owner Don Hudson even formed a club, the Qualifiers, with members such as Bart Root and Hank Rootlieb, who met there. And he started a sideline buying basket cases and building them into nice rods to sell, complete with cool upholstery. The photo of the orange 1929 roadster was taken around 1960, when employee Darrell "Whitey" Morgan took over the shop. What's that ratty-looking 1932 roadster in the garage doorway in early 1956? That's the earliest known photo of the Deuce that became Tom McMullen's, shortly after Hudson got it in pieces and had club member John Beerfeldt start assembling it.

Don finished the Deuce in shiny black lacquer, a chopped windshield, split chromed radius rods, a chromed and drilled front axle, a hot flathead, and nice black and white tuck-and-roll. As such it got one photo in the December 1956 *HRM* while appearing on *The Life of Riley* TV show. Then he sold it to a high school kid in Norwalk, Chuck Karnatz, who added the bobbed rear fenders, as seen here. There was at least one more owner, who installed a small-block Chevy adapted to the early Ford driveline, before McMullen bought it. This is how it looked when he got the car.

I have shown photos of Art Chrisman's renowned No. 25 dragster in various forms and eras throughout this book. I know it was at the ribbon-cutting of the first NHRA Nationals drags in Great Bend, Kansas, in 1955, running a Chrysler Hemi that destroyed the early Ford trans. It also briefly ran a Y-block engine as part of a FoMoCo team at Daytona Beach. However, sometime before 1957, as Art was building *Hustler I*, this is how No. 25 looked: a pile of parts pushed into a corner. It was all obsolete, so thankfully nothing was sold off. More thankfully, Art still had it, and was able to beautifully rebuild it (and run it) twenty-five years later.

Chapter Six Early Hot Rod Shops and Speed Parts

I'm cheating on this one. I think it's the only photo in this book I took myself, so it's not from the 1950s or 1960s. If you love vintage hot rod parts, this is to die for. It was on the workbench in Ohio George Montgomery's speed shop outside Dayton the first time I went out there to see it and meet George. Yes, it's a *pair* of Zora Arkus-Duntov V-8-60 Ardun baby hemi engines, complete. These are out of maybe six known to exist. And they weren't even the rarest or coolest things I saw in his shop on the day of my unannounced visit. That's all I can say.

"If you love vintage hot rod parts, this is to die for."

No, this isn't a case of "If one blower is good, two are better." This was a singular case of Ted "Doc" Rawleigh employing the mechanical advantage of dual-stage supercharging (used on World War II aircraft), with a 6-71 compressing air into a 4-71, which further compressed it before pumping the charge into an Olds engine to make 670 hp on gas in 1960. Not bad. But given the small slicks of the time, the short ltow chassis, and the added weight of the Jimmy blowers, there was no way to put that power to the ground, and I've never seen another example.

Hot Rod Gallery   141

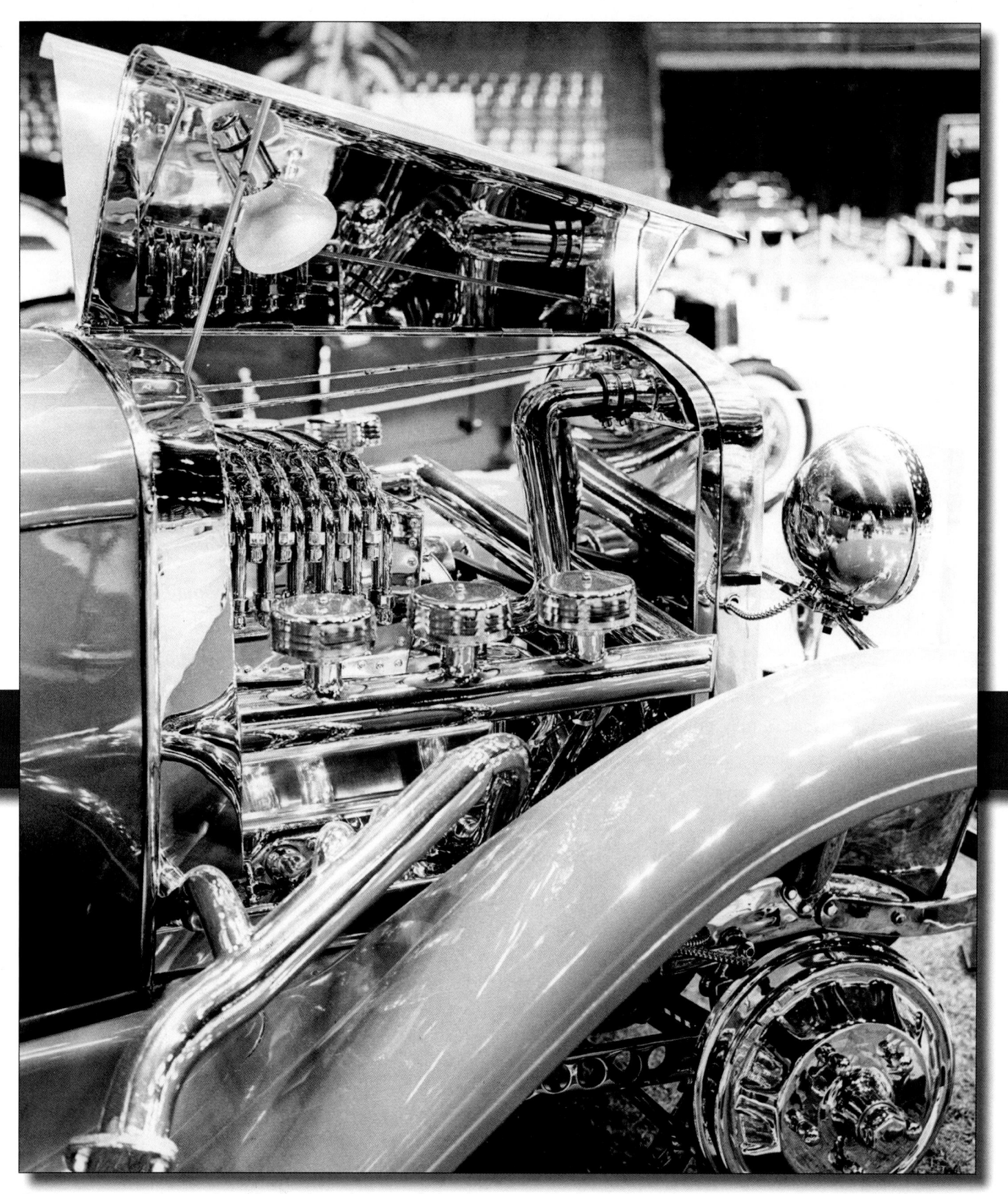

This last piece of chromed mechanical monkey-puzzle leads appropriately into Chapter Seven. Yes, it's a striking photo of the unidentifiable engine in the *Alazan* Model A show coupe. Not only is nearly everything (frame, brakes, under-fenders, underhood, firewall, radiator) chrome plated, but that maze of chrome tubing and air cleaners was meant to mystify onlookers and make judges count points. It was actually ducting created by owner Howard Mitchell to route air from a Paxton blower into a 1957 Lincoln mill. I last saw this car in Colorado in 1992, powered by—what else?—a 350 Chevy.

CHAPTER SEVEN

Car Shows, Angel Hair and Tiki Heads

I'm not a big fan of car shows. Oh, I like to go see them, with all the beautifully painted, polished, and chromed cars proudly displayed under bright lights. You can casually stroll through and stop and study the ones you like down to small details in the engine, interior, or undercarriage because they're propped up with the wheels off, everything open, and even mirrors underneath to show off every spotless square inch. I can ignore most of the sideshow of bands, beauty contests, auctions, and the seemingly ever-present Batmobile incarnation with third-tier TV stars signing glossy photos. The candy-colored cars (and motorcycles, and boats, and . . .) in every type, shape, and age create more than enough carnival spectacle to fully entertain me. Especially if I can go and wander around, stay as long as I want, then leave when I'm ready.

What I don't care for is entering my car in a show. I've done it enough times over the years to know what I'm talking about. The first problem is getting the car there and back. I'm talking about the usual indoor car show that starts on Friday night and runs through an interminable trophy presentation on Sunday evening. That means you've somehow got to get the car there, leave it, then come back to get it. You have several options here, but none are fun. Especially considering most car shows are held in the dead of winter. If you've done it, you know.

The second problem is that you need some sort of display. That means you have to make it, get it there along with your car, set it up, take it back down, and get it all home. Of course you could just park your car on the show floor and let it speak for itself. But then you'd lose points for not displaying details; if your hood, doors, or trunk aren't open, those areas aren't even judged. In addition, you get judged for more points on the display itself. This is especially significant for the period I'm showing.

Third, and most significant, is that these car shows became competitions. That's what this chapter is really about. My idea of a really fun car show is the one-day affair (indoor or out). You drive your car there, park it where they tell you, let them put a rope around it with a small sign with your name and city written on it, then

"Getting a car finished to the point that I finally consider it nice enough to enter a car show is reward enough."

polish it up a bit, spend the rest of the day looking at the other cool cars, and visiting with your friends. Then you drive home that afternoon in your nice, clean car. For me, getting a car finished to the point that I finally consider it nice enough to *enter* a car show is reward enough.

With the advent of judged rod and custom car shows in the early 1950s (with classes, points, and trophies), certain owners, builders, and professional shops either couldn't control their competitive spirit or saw it as a way to gain some fame (that is, get their picture in a magazine) or generate some business. The problem was, and still is, that judging custom cars is subjective. It's not like a drag race that has a definite winner.

Given the points system adopted almost universally by the new promoters and their judges, it soon became more quantitative. You could rack up more points and win a bigger trophy if you had more modifications to the body, more speed parts on the engine, more chrome on the chassis, more custom upholstery, more intricate paint, and even a more elaborate display. Maybe. You couldn't be sure, because there was still that subjective element. You figured that if you didn't win this time, you needed to do more: more paint, more chrome, more carburetors, more scoops to try to win the next time.

On top of that, even if you did win, some promoters actually required that you make a certain number of major modifications to your car before you could enter it in the same show the next year. Their thinking was that the public wouldn't pay to see the same cars they saw the year before.

By the late 1950s car shows were increasingly competitive, and also more commercial. The same was happening in drag racing. The shows' promoters wanted to make

Whether it's between George Barris and his brother Sam, or between George and his contemporary customizers, there's no question who was the showman extraordinaire. It's my guess that George was as intent on outdoing himself as he was winning trophies. The *Golden Sahara*, built from his own wrecked/decapitated 1953 Lincoln, was his first mega show car, seen here in 1957 at some sort of debut (and photo op) at the Ford plant in Commerce, California, in 1957. That's metal-man Bill Ortega (aka DeCarr) next to George. Owner Jim Skonzakis (aka Street, sitting in the car) of Ohio was at least as ambitious as George, having the car completely rebuilt from jet age to space age by 1960.

---

money and they had to draw a crowd. The audiences at these shows wanted to see something special: match racing "name" dragsters, the show custom from the latest magazine cover, or a hot rod seen on a national TV show. It had to be a spectacle. The not-so-surprising part was how willing and eager the car owners/builders were to join this competition fest. Soon both rods and customs that were driven on the street were modified to the point that they were only legal to run on drag strips, or they were too painted, polished, chromed, and upholstered to venture on a highway. Then there were show cars that the owners wouldn't even start for fear of turning an exhaust pipe blue or leaking gas out of a carburetor. It went further than that. But I don't need to tell you. Just look at the pictures.

Chapter Seven *Car Shows, Angel Hair and Tiki Heads*

While the *Sahara* was more a concept car, Bill Carr's *Aztec* 1956 Chevy was more a culmination of the competitive custom cars Barris had been building through the 1950s. It made the cover of *HRM* in August 1958. With its quad lights, chopped cantilever roof, and multiple sculpted scoops, it took the tail-dragging, skirted, Appleton spotlight-style custom to its limits. However, note that it's still sitting with its wheels on the ground and its hood shut. Things soon went from sublime to ridiculous.

Here's a prime example of a street rod becoming a show car and creating a professional career for its owner/builder. This is Squeeg Jerger's candy apple red Deuce coupe at the Cleveland Autorama in 1961. You can see the big trophies it's already won thanks to its flawless paint, white undercarriage, chrome suspension/firewall/engine, and details such as brake scoops and tuck-and-roll running boards. Squeeg's Kustoms is still going strong in Chandler, Arizona.

Hot Rod Gallery 145

While other street rods were being turned into drag machines, what better to do with a quickly outmoded dragster than to turn it into a show car? Seen at the 1960 Omaha show, the Saints club's blown Olds rail with six carburetors and a solid front axle was not only obsolete, but also actually outlawed by then. Nevertheless, it won First Place and Best Engineered trophies in the dragster class. The display with grass carpet and live potted palms undoubtedly helped.

Things aren't getting too crazy yet, but the open exhaust, six carbs, four headlights, and little upholstered running boards were added to Dale Schott's short-bed 1929 roadster at the 1960 Columbus, Ohio, Autorama for show, not go. Also note the chrome firewall, double-sided whitewalls, and handmade wheel covers covered in Naugahyde.

146 Chapter Seven *Car Shows, Angel Hair and Tiki Heads*

"Not only does the tinfoil and angel hair display add points, but so does the 'safety equipment.'"

Okay, here's what's happening. This 1956 T-Bird seen at the 1960 Hartford Autorama isn't radically customized, but it has been "detailed" a little more each year (chrome suspension and brakes, upholstery everywhere, even outside) so it has morphed from a street-driver to a show-only car. Not only does the tinfoil and angel hair display add points, but so does the "safety equipment," whether in the trunk or on the floor.

Now it's getting ridiculous. This is the Midstates Show in Evansville, Indiana, in 1960. You probably didn't recognize this car with the canted chrome horns and tuck-and-roll roof as a 1932 Ford roadster. It's somewhat overshadowed by fake palms, grass, moss, ferns, and lily pads in a real water fountain tumbling into a rock pool: good for a big Best Display trophy. Anything not painted or upholstered white pearl on the car appears to be chromed. But the crowning touch was "more than 2,000 hand-set rhinestones and pearls" glued on the body in pinstripe-like designs.

Hot Rod Gallery 147

> "Bow-tied Ray Goodwin looks very pleased with his take at the 1961 Atlanta Rod and Custom Show."

So what compelled people to do this with automobiles? Some glittery trophies in various sizes handed out by a buxom show queen wearing a sash, a tiara, and a bathing suit. Bow-tied Ray Goodwin looks very pleased with his take at the 1961 Atlanta Rod and Custom Show, including Best Display, Best Comp, Most Popular, and Best in Show. His car? Don't know. There wasn't a photo of it in my file.

Here's a rare example of a show car that got better, not worse. Chili Catallo's Olds-powered Deuce coupe started out on the street, and then went drag racing with a Paxton blower. It's seen here with its sharp-dressed and smiling owner at the 1960 Detroit Autorama as customized in a very modern style by the Alexander Brothers. Next, it went west to get a chopped top and pearl blue paint at the Barris shop, which not only got it on the cover of *HRM*, but also on the famous Beach Boys album, *Little Deuce Coupe*.

Chapter Seven *Car Shows, Angel Hair and Tiki Heads*

Did I mention angel hair and palm trees? Also note the hand-carved wooden Tiki head atop the radiator of Allen Crosby's 1927 T in Houston. The best part of this car is the Tri-Power 348 engine. However, the mesh over the radiator wouldn't help drivability, and the tarp over the interior cost points (it might be hiding upholstery that wasn't done yet). Remember, this was the era when young, bearded Bob Denver was playing Maynard G. Krebs on *Dobie Gillis*.

"The best part of this car is the Tri-Power 348 engine."

Tony Krajacic's 1929 roadster might have looked good when the flathead engine, full moon wheel covers, and wide whitewalls were in style a decade earlier. But as seen here in 1960 in Columbus, Ohio, with molded headlights/hood, side aprons with chrome pipes, ugly fenders, and pastel pink paint, I can't say its looks have been improved by the modifications. Yet it won seventeen Best in Show trophies and got on a couple of magazine covers. Go figure.

Hot Rod Gallery 149

It would be very interesting to know about the origins, and the future, of this partially finished contraption shown at the Hartford Autorama in 1961. Likely inspired by Ed Roth's *Outlaw*, I'd guess the finned body was made of fiberglass. Not only is the complete early-Ford rear end chromed, but so is the front (including brake drums and shoes!), as well as the hole-cut frame. The headerless Pontiac engine has a beltless GMC blower mounted on top. I wonder if it was ever finished, ran, or driven. I doubt it. I do like the grass carpet, little picket fence, and plastic roses.

This seriously dressed guy is a show judge at the Hartford Autorama. He has a list of potential points-grabbing details, and he's checking them off. This custom 1957 Chevy with Cadillac fins has a wet bar, built-in TV set, chrome tools, and a kitchen stove cooking clam chowder . . . and that's just in its tuck-and-rolled trunk. I'd bet the matching upholstered modern stools counted, too. I have no idea whether this show-winning machine looked good or not, but see the giant trophies displayed next to it? That's what it was built to do, and it obviously did it well.

Chapter Seven *Car Shows, Angel Hair and Tiki Heads*

Another big trophy the promoters cooked up was Best Club Display, which generated more enthusiasm. The Kustom Kings were chosen as "hosts" of the 1961 Cleveland show, but realized they only had one finished car. So they devised an ingenious display titled "How a Show Car is Built," starting with a chassis and working up to the finished car. This required lots of angel hair, tinfoil, and fishnets to cover unfinished portions. Jerry Roman's 1953 Olds hardtop depicted Stage 2, which apparently meant chrome plating everything from the firewall forward, including the towbar and, yes, the brake shoes. This was the era when "leadsleds" had given way to "custom by chrome."

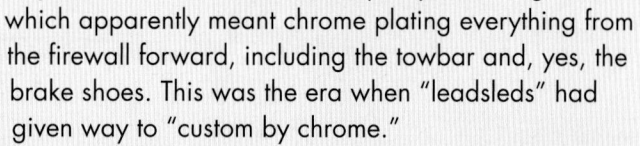

In the early days custom builders had plush, comfortable, tuck-and-roll upholstery installed to make the interior look more luxurious and inviting. Given what competitive show car builders were doing to the rest of their cars to increase points to win trophies, you can imagine what they cooked up for the insides (and elsewhere, in many cases). Of course it started with more: more tuck-and-roll, more colors. Soon it incorporated custom-built seats, plastic shift knobs and grab rails, telephones, record players, wet bars, you name it. This 1957 Chev combines vinyl and velour, tuck-and-roll and button-tuft, and some furry angora. Plush and luxurious? No. Eyeball grabbing? Yes!

Hot Rod Gallery   151

"This is an egregious example of too much of a good thing."

Although you see some tiger stripes on the dash of this 1957 Ford, it's a little less garish. But this is an egregious example of too much of a good thing. The small amount that isn't covered in tuck-and-roll is chrome plated.

"Of course it started with more: more tuck-and-roll, more colors."

Considering that this candy cane upholstery is in the cramped confines of a chopped and heavily channeled 1934 coupe, I'd hate to think what might happen to occupants closed in there on a long trip, such as acute schizophrenia. Don't worry, this car wasn't going any farther than being pushed on and off the show floor.

Chapter Seven *Car Shows, Angel Hair and Tiki Heads*

> "The next stage was creating wild, custom, swiveling seats for even wilder upholstery."

The next stage, beyond covering everything in wild tuck-and-roll patterns, was creating wild, custom, swiveling seats for even wilder upholstery. These button-tufted loungers were created by Carl Casper for his annually evolving *Exotic Empress*, a chopped, hard-topped, canted-quad-headlight 1950 Chevy that had all the bells, bullets, and whistles (and matching upholstery in the wheel wells, under the hood, and in the trunk). It still only placed second in the first International Championship show car series in 1961. Nevertheless, it did launch a career for Casper, both as a builder and show promoter.

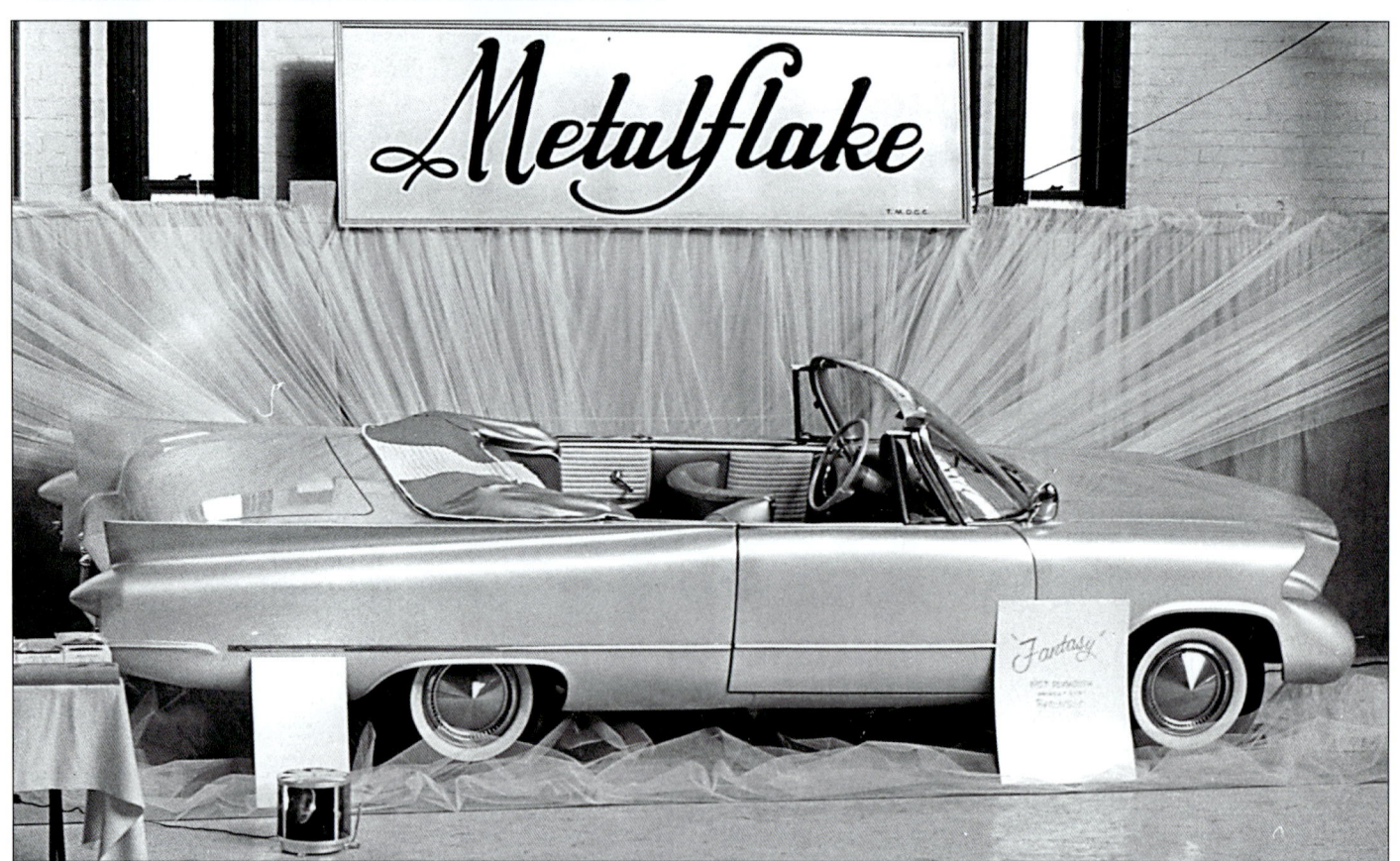

You might notice that the show cars in this chapter don't have the frenzied flames or scallops seen in Chapter Six. They were too quick and easy. You had to have a full, serious, multi-layer paint job such as candy, pearl, or something even more difficult and arcane. Enter Metalflake, introduced by the Dobeckman Company in 1960. It was basically glitter you could spray through a gun. It was tricky to do and very hard to get smooth. But it made show-goers (and judges) gape, gasp, and have to touch. This sparkly silver display vehicle, surrounded by billowing taffeta, is "a 1957 Plymouth convertible with a Stude Lark hood and grille, 1959 Buick rear quarters, 1937 Plymouth headlight housings, custom taillights, and swiveling chairs for front seats."

Hot Rod Gallery   153

Don't think that I had to dig through my files of late-1950s to early-1960s car shows to find these few outlandish examples of overdone show cars. Just the opposite. These samples are truly typical. The pleasant surprise was finding a few nice rods or customs residing on angel hair scattered in the mix. One of them is this beautiful, very low, candy red 1940 sedan of Barry Hutchings displayed at a 1960 show in Vancouver, British Columbia. The chrome wheels, molded 1950 taillights, small nerfs, plus quad lights and contemporary flames in front all give it a slightly more modern look. A McCulloch-blown Buick V-8 even earned it extra show points. The stance, despite the angel hair, is what makes this one totally cool.

Once you get past the palm trees and picket fence, you might notice that very little has been done to this Cameo pickup other than paint and upholstery, but both are done to extreme. Panel painting, with carefully fogged candy color around the edges of taped-off panel designs, was the hot new style promulgated by Larry Watson, Dick Jackson, and Ed Roth. You'll note that even the doorjambs have fogged panels. Moreover, the reason it has rolls everywhere, from pedals to tailgate, is because it was built and entered by an upholstery shop.

Chapter Seven *Car Shows, Angel Hair and Tiki Heads*

"Once the finned 1957 factory cars came out, the show car customizers had to outdo them, of course. Bigger, better."

Customizers got into the jet-age tailfin thing well before Detroit caught on. Once the finned 1957 factory cars came out, the show car customizers had to outdo them, of course. Bigger, better. Believe it or not, Anthony Abato's *Comet* from Jersey City was a 1954 Oldsmobile. However, Continental kits and chrome stars weren't considered cool. Ray Czuba's *Lime Rickey* from Cleveland simply exaggerated the fins on his 1957 DeSoto. Check out the sculpturing and taillight on the primered Ford Vicky in the background.

Tommy Ivo has always been the consummate showman: exactly what any drag strip or car show promoter could hope for. And what better than a bright red dragster with four fuel-injected Buick engines powering four giant slicks, with chrome pipes sticking out everywhere, to draw in and awe an admiring crowd? Better yet, Tommy was also a minor TV star, and had just appeared on the full cover of *HRM*. What I love about this low-angle photo is that it's really a snap portrait of the young, multi-faceted audience checking out the car (or cameraman).

Is this a hot rod? A custom car? What exactly is it? It's an extremely rare 1932 Ford roadster pickup that Ray Fahrner had his custom shop completely rework into this swoopy, toothy, pearl blue and white button-tufted show rod, in the style set by the Barris *Ala Kart* that won the big Oakland trophy in 1958–1959. Seen at a 1960 show, a small sign notes that this car is "For Display Only." Rather than vying for trophies, it was presented as an example of the shop's quality workmanship, with the hope of generating customers. The fact that the promoter likely paid a lot for it to appear as a "Feature Car" further removed the need to compete.

156 Chapter Seven *Car Shows, Angel Hair and Tiki Heads*

Lee Wells was a custom upholsterer from Davenport, Iowa, who built some pretty wild show cars primarily to demonstrate his stitching talents. As seen here in his chopped 1958 Ranchero, he could not only tuck-and-roll and button-tuft with the best of 'em, but he could sculpt seats and dashboards, too. It had similar upholstery in the bed, in the wheel wells, and even in the grille.

The *Ala Kart*, Farhner's *Eclipse*, and Krikorian's *Emperor*. The wild new show rods of 1960 were all built from real Ford roadster bodies that were highly customized. But Ed "Big Daddy" Roth blew the lid off in his inimitable way with the *Outlaw*, which he literally hand-built from nothing more than an old Cadillac engine, some metal frame rails, and sculpted fiberglass. Built in 1959 and debuting on the January 1960 *Car Craft* cover, it at least bore a resemblance to a hot rod. But it opened the floodgates for zany "anything on wheels" show machines to come.

"Roth built them so he could dazzle young kids at shows and sell them T-shirts, decals, and other trinkets . . . which he did quite successfully."

Just one year later Roth trumped himself with the bubble-topped *Beatnik Bandit.* To give a small idea of the "Wow!" factor of these cars at the time, mega-promoter Bob Larivee bought both cars and featured them at all his shows across the country. Revell sold millions of models of them. I can vouch that neither has ever been driven on a street, even though they do run. And as far as I know, neither has ever won a trophy. Roth built them so he could dazzle young kids at shows and sell them T-shirts, decals, and other trinkets . . . which he did quite successfully. Thank goodness both are preserved in museums.

CHAPTER EIGHT

1950s Hot Rods in Color

Have you ever seen the original 1939 movie The Wizard of Oz, in which Judy Garland was an innocent teenager playing wide-eyed Dorothy? If you actually saw it at a theater, rather than on your old black-and-white TV, then you should remember how dramatically the movie changed from black-and-white to full-on Technicolor once Dorothy and Toto's drab Kansas farmhouse landed in Oz. That's sort of what's happening right here in this book.

At the beginning, I apologized that so much of this photo collection was black-and-white. Given the decades I'm covering, that was the reality of photography. Especially for amateurs, who took most of the photos in preceding chapters, black-and-white was the only film choice. When the availability of color film increased, it required better cameras and more expensive processing. Even then you got slides, which required a projector and screen to view them.

On the other hand, I don't want to downplay or belittle the wonderful black-and-white photos you've seen so far. I'm a big fan of black-and-white photography, especially of the Ansel Adams, Edward Weston, Dorothea Lange, and Robert Frank sort. It's the type of photography I do myself, when I'm not working. I'm certainly not comparing the preceding chapters of this book to the drab, gray, dust bowl Kansas of Dorothy and Toto.

These last two chapters explode with color in a perfectly fitting 1950s way. It was certainly a colorful era. The hot rods, custom cars, and drag machines of that era were colorful in all of the meanings of the word. So were the people who owned, built, drove, and posed in these pictures with them. Their clothes and hairstyles, as well as the backgrounds or settings of the photos themselves, all add to a multi-faceted portrait of the time and culture. All that's missing is the soundtrack.

Admittedly there wasn't as much color film being shot in the early 1950s as there was in the latter half of the decade. Furthermore, some of these images do stray into the early 1960s (1962 at the latest), but I think you'll agree that they belong more with the 1950s. The big change for hot rods came in 1962 with the introduction of muscle cars, Super Stocks, and other big-inch, multi-carb, four-speed "factory hot rods" that you could

> "These last two chapters explode with color in a perfectly fitting 1950s way. It was certainly a colorful era."

buy new in the showroom and drive straight to the dragstrip to race. By 1965 the kind of hot rods shown here evaporated from magazine covers. They were replaced first by dragsters, Altereds, then Funny Cars, dune buggies, boats, and finally vans. Culturally the big shift came about the same time: clothing, hair, the music, and so much more. That's a topic for another time and place.

I could say a lot more about the images shown here, but the last thing I want to mention is that these are all original photographs (known as color transparencies, or large-format "slides") that I have preserved in my files for decades. In all cases, this film is at least fifty years old. The Ektachrome film that was used back then has a tendency to "color shift" with time. That means it not only fades, but also loses its green tones and takes on a reddish or magenta hue. Fortunately it only happens in certain cases, and most of these photos have preserved quite well. As you probably know, today's computer technology allows for all sorts of enhancement or manipulation of photographs, but I will do only a limited amount of selective "color correction" to restore the colors to more correct hues. So even if a few of these photos look a little

On the October 1953 *R&C* cover, Dick Bundick's V-8-60-powered 1932 three-window is bright yellow. But its color isn't mentioned, and my guess is it was added by the printer (yes, they could "photo-doctor" even then). But the real story of this dynamic shot is told by editor Spence in a funny sidebar about how they located Miss Modesto to pose, and then had her sister pour buckets of water on her to keep her wet.

---

on the faded side, I hope you'll agree with me that they are wonderful, classic images of a long-gone era that we still love. Even if they've aged a bit, thankfully, we still have them to appreciate.

Chapter Eight *1950s Hot Rods in Color*

Roy Desbrow's chopped, channeled, and shortened 1932 Ford pickup with a sectioned hood and grille not only made the color cover of the January 1952 *HRM*, but also got a full Rex Burnett cutaway inside. The truck had bodywork by a friend and upholstery by Bob Lee. Roy drove it to work at Mitchell Muffler in Pasadena.

I love this photo so much I have a framed print of it hanging on my garage wall. Young Don Van Hoff built this chopped, four-carb flathead-powered Deuce five-window while he was in high school, even keeping it a secret from his dad. For some strange reason they changed its colors on the December 1955 *HRM* cover, but I think the pink and green split-level house adds as much to this photo as Don and his hot rod.

> "You can tell by his hat and his license that Jim Govro and the *Tweety Bird*, his channeled 1932, are from Texas."

You can tell by his hat and his license that Jim Govro and the *Tweety Bird*, his channeled '32, are from Texas. It's unusual in retaining stock fenders; these are nicely bobbed where the running boards were removed. Somebody got up on something high to get this striking photo. The only info I could find was one picture from a drag meet, where the *Tweety Bird* from Austin was running a roll bar and 1950 Cadillac mill in the B/Street Roadster class.

If you want the full story on Dave Cunningham's deeply channeled, candy red Forty sedan, including where it is and what it looks like today, I highly recommend my own recent CarTech book, *Lost Hot Rods II*. This is its first version as seen on several magazine covers in 1958, mainly because its "special mix red" lacquer really looked like candy, even when printed on cheap magazine paper. This fat 1940 looked much better with its body lowered, fenders and grille raised, and hood sectioned, than it would if the top were chopped, but it's one of the few that got this treatment. Plus, Cunningham was a good, enthusiastic photographer.

This classic drive-in photo, with the uniformed waitress, window tray, and period-perfect red Deuce coupe staged at the famous Bob's Big Boy was so good I made a blow-up of it and mounted it on the wall of a special hot rod show I did years ago in the art gallery at Art Center College in Pasadena. One evening an older gentleman stopped at it and said, loudly, "Hey that's my car!" It was Elton McEldowney, who still lived nearby. He told me that he was a cook at the Pasadena Bob's drive-in in 1957 when the coupe was featured in a small cover photo and two pages inside the June issue. It says he's a chef, but neither this photo nor any mention of Bob is included. It's a great photo; excellent Deuce coupe; strange story.

Hot Rod Gallery   163

This is a fun comparison. Of course the fuel-injected Buick in the Titian Red T is Tommy Ivo's, complete with Von Dutch pinstriping, circa 1957. It's inarguably one of the two most famous T-Buckets ever. The carbureted version is how Bill Rolland "spiffed it up" to turn it into a show rod in 1961. Later Barris redid it again for Hy Rosen. My one question here is: Why don't the four-bar radius rod ends have nuts on them in the Ivo version?

"The young guy with the wavy red hair is Neal East."

The young guy with the wavy red hair is Neal East, and this cobalt blue chopped Deuce five-window with the gold Olds mill, which he built with help from his dad, was his first of several magazine cover cars (April 1958 *HRM*). Neal became a staffer at *R&C*, owned the gold 1932 Roadster seen on its first full-size cover, also owned and drove the famed Doane Spencer Deuce for years, and operated two automotive bookstores, plus he's still building and driving hot rods cross-country today.

Chapter Eight *1950s Hot Rods in Color*

Black cars have always been difficult to photograph. But placing this one against a backdrop of pink and red flowers to pick up the red wheels and interior, as well as having the white road surface reflecting light from below, makes this one work perfectly, especially since it's complemented by owner Jack Thompson's big white smile. Unfortunately by 1958, when this photo was taken, its wire wheels, skinny black tires, and beautifully formed track roadster panels were passé. Thankfully, however, the car was preserved and has been meticulously restored by Gary and Karen Schroeder, who still make track-style steering gear in Burbank, California.

> "Running more than 130 mph on gas, it afforded little protection between the driver's derriere and the tarmac."

The only thing wrong with this low-angle photo is that you might think the front of the car extends to normal dragster length. No. The front wheels are just out of the picture. The Bob's Muffler Coburn & Crowe dragster of 1959 was an early, successful rear-engine car, and the beginning of the feared Ridge Route Terrors team. It was also little more than a Chrysler Hemi-powered go-kart. Running more than 130 mph on gas, it afforded little protection between the driver's derriere and the tarmac, as this striking photo shows.

This is another of my favorite hot rod photos. The cut-down 1927 T roadster with its upswept chrome side pipes looks like a totally fun car, and the young crew-cut guy and blonde gal are obviously enjoying it. The owner, Bob Smith, was a sailor in San Diego, and his "friend" Bonnie was actually his sister. The story that accompanied its feature in the March 1958 *HRM* said how affordable building a similar roadster could be because its components were, in essence, obsolete. One thing I noticed was the car had no license plates, and then it just vanished. I've never seen anything exactly like it since. Why not?

Hot Rod Gallery   165

I remember well seeing this pair of "magazine cars" in local shows when I was a kid. The selling point was that Ron Coleman built them in his home garage, and he and his wife each drove them. The channeled coupe had a rolled rear pan, and the hardtop-chopped 1951 Ford had 1953 Olds 98 rear quarters. We'd call it a perfect hot rod family garage today. But back in 1960 (when this photo was taken), a flathead-powered deuce and a full-custom shoebox in this style were rarities.

This a wild, colorful roadster in a dynamic front-yard setting with two guys in equally colorful car club jackets "working" on it. The young owner on the far side, John Rasmussen, was later partners with me (and Gene Adams) in a dragster. Fittingly, this roadster was soon converted to Olds OHV power, and "Rass" went on to field several successful Top Fuel rails.

Chapter Eight *1950s Hot Rods in Color*

Why would I feature a photo of a cool hot rod from the rear with its trunk open? First, taken from this high angle, it grabs your attention. Second, you don't expect a car's trunk to be elaborately upholstered in white and red tuck-and-roll, complete with custom pockets for accessories. And third, the whole rear of this car is customized with a rolled pan, bobbed fenders, Pontiac taillights, and a chrome-tube nerf bar. This 1960 showpiece was owned by Portland's Bob and Terry Tindle, who trumped it with the incredible *Orange Crate* two years later.

Not only is this a breathtaking car and classic photo, but also it holds more personal meaning for me than I can tell here. I saw the Geraghty & Crawford *Grasshopper* on the cover of *HRM*, October 1959; I bought and built several of the Monogram model kits. Then I saw it run at Fontana Drag City. When I moved to Glendale twenty-five years ago, I took my car to Geraghty Automotive to have it dyno tuned. Finally, a few years ago I was able to interview John at his home for a feature profile in *The Rodder's Journal*. John Geraghty is now a renowned collector and curator of western art.

> "I also spot a Tony Nancy decal on the stock-height windshield, attesting to the quality of the blue and white pleated interior."

This photo is pure fun. The 1927 T roadster belongs to Dale Gould, the kid with grease on his hands. You can see the white-detailed Olds engine has six chrome-topped 97s on a polished log manifold, and despite the tow-bar tabs welded on the dropped axle, it has at least been driven enough to turn the chrome headers blue. I also spot a Tony Nancy decal on the stock-height windshield, attesting to the quality of the blue and white pleated interior.

> "The 394 Olds was in Jim Seaton's 1929 A drag roadster."

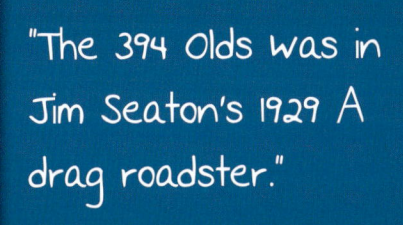

The August 1960 *HRM* cover was a patchwork of fourteen photos. One of those was a left-side view of this Olds engine with a Potvin front-drive, two-port Hilborn–injected, polished 6-71 GMC blower. There's a similar shot inside in an article on "big engines," but no details. I can tell you the 394 Olds was in Jim Seaton's 1929 A drag roadster, and the photo was surprisingly taken by Griff Borgeson, a highly respected automotive journalist who was, by 1960, much more interested in European classics.

168 Chapter Eight *1950s Hot Rods in Color*

You saw Chili Catallo with his black, unchopped Deuce coupe in Chapter Seven on page 147. Here it is in its much more famous chopped version with blue and white pearl paint by Junior Conway at the Barris shop, circa 1961. But neither the July *HRM* cover, with Chili behind the car, nor the Beach Boys' *Little Deuce Coupe* album cover, which ignominiously chopped his head off, is nearly as dynamic as this one, which I think was instigated (or actually taken) by Ed Roth, who gave it to me. Ed also gave Chili his bright red jacket ("to liven up the picture"); if you look really closely, you'll see Ed's name embroidered on it.

"Two supercharged gas engines ran faster than one."

As I've mentioned, when the NHRA banned nitro fuel in the late 1950s, it didn't take dragster builders long to figure out that two supercharged gas engines ran faster than one. It also made for dramatic photos, especially when taken head-on from a high angle, like this. It helps even more when the blowers are mounted out front, with dual Hilborn injectors between them, making for a mechanical menagerie of pipes, tubes, chrome, aluminum, and paint. This is the Dragmaster *Two Thing* in 1961.

The one strange thing about Larry Ready's metallic mint green 1929 A coupe is the chrome 1927 T radiator shell, but even that works. Other details such as the pearl white tuck-and-roll top and running boards, dressed and chromed T-Bird Y-block, bobbed rear fenders, and chrome reversed wheels with baldy caps mounting medium big-and-little whitewalls (yes, that's possible) are all right on. Coincidentally or not, today Ready is a member of the Los Angeles Roadsters, as is the car's current owner Jeff Tann.

"That shifter is part of a pogo stick."

With its candy burgundy metal-flake paint, jade mist upholstery, and pinstriped candy green dash, it's surprising that no color photos (nor the Tiki-hut background) were used when *Rod & Custom* devoted four pages to this 1926 T in one of its first Road Tests in the May 1962 issue. Owner Gary Heliker did his own bodywork and paint on the original-steel, Buick-powered roadster. Burgundy and green? Tiki heads? By the way, that shifter is part of a pogo stick. It all works. Where did this one go?

Chapter Eight *1950s Hot Rods in Color*

Although the car was owned by his brother Bob, that's Terry Tindle on the left with Everett Lorenzen. This photo is from "the piercing camera of Pete Sukalac" as stated in the February 1962 *HRM*. Pete was a prolific freelancer from Portland who shared photos with me and even taught me how to take pictures at car shows. The car, of course, is the incomparable *Orange Crate*, which both Terry and Everett drove at drag races before Bob made it a serious show car (note completely chromed tube frame). It won the Oakland Roadster Show (and many other shows), was on the cover of *HRM*, and was also made into a Revell model kit that is still available. When this long-lost car appeared at the Deuce 75th Anniversary show, body tilted and in mostly original condition I, along with everybody else present, was pleasantly astounded.

Can you tell these guys are brothers, and that they're having a good time? Have you noticed that most of the people in these pictures look like they're having fun? That's the point. That's what this whole hot rodding thing is about. The driver is Bob Urquhart, who found the 1927 T body in the desert and built the 276-inch DeSoto Hemi–powered T at home in San Diego, with help from brother Norm, the passenger. You might notice a small Prowlers club plaque under the rear deck.

Another San Diego rod, the Jackman brothers' candy wild cherry 1932 sport coupe, has a license plate, but even it is chromed. So is the entire frame, which they had to cut in half to fit into the chrome tanks, and then bolt back together. The brothers (Tom and Harry) made the floor of clear plexiglass so all the chrome underneath (including eight full-length exhaust pipes with no mufflers) could be seen. Winning all those trophies is what this rod was about, a different kind of fun. The Jackman family story (they once owned Halibrand, among other things) would make a book. Harry Jackman built an exact clone of this car for the 75th Anniversary, and then the real one showed up, too!

Chapter Eight *1950s Hot Rods in Color*

> "This car was Tony's brief transition piece to full-on dragsters."

This is the multi-talented Tony Nancy at his upholstery/race car shop in Sherman Oaks with the third, fast, supercharged, bright orange drag roadster in a row that made the cover of *HRM*. The beautifully detailed Buick nailhead engine with the 6-71 GMC blower and "barn door" Enderle injector was his hallmark during this period. Actually this car, classed as a Modified Roadster with a minimal fiberglass replica T body, was Tony's brief transition piece to full-on dragsters.

I think this is a wonderful photo for several reasons. First, the way it's composed, the way it's lit, and the colors make it a good photograph. Second, three guys working on a car in their driveway is all-American hot rodding, especially 1950s-style; plus, the steep angle adds to the impact. Third, again, it's a picture of having fun. Brothers Pat and Mike Germon, with older brother-in-law Bob Ahlstrom (who painted it) built the roadster pickup with T and Dodge body parts and a wood bed on a 1932 frame. Although it was photographed in 1962, the 1950 flathead, 1932 shell, and steel wheels with hubcaps and whitewalls make it very much a 1950s-style rod.

Hot Rod Gallery   173

I've loved this chopped, blown-Chrysler, candy tangerine, wicked-looking 1934 drag coupe since I first saw it in the October 1962 issue of *HRM*. The polished 12-spokes, the bare chrome grille, and especially the amber-tinted windows all add to "the look." A few years ago when I came across these photos and reread the story (which shows the big blown Hemi hooked to a 1939 Ford trans), I figured this machine was for show, not go. Somehow I found owner Sheldon Schmidt, who told me, "That was just to get it in a magazine so I could get sponsors." He rebuilt the car for serious racing, but it eventually ended up upside-down on the golf course across the street from the end of the Pomona drag strip!

Tony Spicola, a freelance photographer from Colorado, had the touch for making young ladies in bathing suits standing next to hot rods in the middle of nowhere seem not only plausible, but also pleasing. In this case, high-heeled Carrlyn Ward's purple suit matches the fogged candy on Jerry Volavka's otherwise pearl white 1931 Fordor. This 1962 feature car was unquestionably a show machine. But looking at its over-chromed three-carb Buick nailhead engine, I've just realized that only one car in this whole chapter has a small-block Chevy in it, and that's a dual-engine dragster. I certainly didn't plan it that way. It's the way these hot rods were in this last golden era.

CHAPTER NINE

1950s Customs in Color

It's fitting that we wrap up this book with a kaleidoscope of color featuring 1950s custom cars. The 1950s was above all a colorful era, and that theme continues here with everything from candy colors and tuck-and-roll, to Tiki heads, palm trees, and bathing beauties. This was the decade that saw the birth of candy apple and pearlescent paints, as well as the shift from deep, luscious, "organic" single-color metallic paint jobs to two-tone, and then three-tone color combinations.

Bold, somewhat crude flame and scallop designs had been used on race cars for decades. Now, the artists used these large, flat-paneled (yet curvaceous) 1950s car bodies as their canvases. Custom painters now began designing and taping-out more flowing sinuous scallop, flame, and pinstripe patterns, and experimenting with candy blends, fades, and fogged designs. This was truly the golden age of custom cars.

It is perhaps surprising to discover that, with only two exceptions, all of the cars shown in this chapter are 1950-vintage vehicles. As I already mentioned, these cars are predominantly base-model low- to mid-range models (Fords to Olds), stripped and shaved of their original identity, then customized into more beautiful and luxurious automobiles using components from high-end vehicles (Packards to Cadillacs).

The kids of the 1930s built hot roadsters out of junkyard parts, and then began to develop this richer, more comfortable custom style in the 1940s using larger post-1935 cars available on used-car lots. By the 1950s, however, everything had changed. This was the postwar era of the baby boom and burgeoning tract-home development. Jobs were plentiful. With a paycheck a young man could easily walk into a dealership and drive out with something new, or nearly new, for "no money down," and "easily affordable payments." They could take these cars directly from the show room to the custom shop.

Likewise, customizers who started in backyards, lean-tos, or one-stall shops quickly expanded into places such as Barris Kustom City, where a team of employees could work on several cars, in various stages, at the same time. The car owner could have customizing done piece-by-piece if he had to drive it to work, or he could leave it at the more spacious shop and pay for the work in installments as it was done. Of course the advent of judged car shows, which began in 1950, fueled a lot of the customizing and re-customizing activity for the car owners and even more so for the competitive, high-profile, and now high-volume shops.

> "The chopped 1949–1951 Mercury is the icon of this custom car generation."

It's difficult to grasp how strong this custom car image is. It's part of our American culture, seemingly equal to that of the hot rod. Yet it flared quickly and brightly and then burned out. Extinguished. Gone.

The chopped 1949–1951 Mercury is the icon of this custom car generation. Yes, a few were chopped and radically customized as brand-new cars. This is the image that comes to mind immediately when anyone says "custom car." In reality, there were only about a dozen of these well-known chopped Mercs during the 1950s. I include just two of them here.

The truth is that the custom car contingent, although seemingly just as strong a part of Americana as the *Kookie Kar* or the *Graffiti Coupe*, has actually always been a much smaller group. The reasons only become obvious when you stop to think about them. To start with, these custom cars cost considerably more than old roadsters or coupes. Doing custom bodywork (forming and welding sheet-metal and paddling lead) takes considerable skill and effort. The same goes for custom painting, especially if you're trying it yourself. If you're paying somebody else to do this work, it's *really* expensive. Just the size of these 1950s customs made a huge difference (with the emphasis on *huge*). Besides bodywork and paint, consider how much one of these full tuck-and-roll upholstery jobs in a 1950 Merc cost, compared to a similar job in a Model A coupe or roadster. See what I mean?

There never were all that many of these gorgeous 1950s customs in the first place. The customs' heyday didn't even survive the decade. To emphasize that statement, consider that the famous Hirohata Merc was bought off the back row of a used-car lot for $500 in 1959, forgotten and unwanted. Why? Car shows were part of it, but it was more because of the radical new designs from Detroit in 1957 through 1960. This coupled with rapidly

Let's start off with something kind of wacky, yet period perfect. Bob Hardee was a uniformed city bus driver by day, but in the 1950s he was the primary freelance rod, custom, and drag race photographer in the San Diego area. He came up with some great cars, settings, and willing participants for his excellent photos. I can't explain the who, where, or why of this one. A two-page feature on Ed Fahlsing's 1950 Ford coupe in the small January 1955 *Car Craft* shows Ed sitting in the car in one full rear photo, plus two close-ups of the round 1953 Olds taillights, and one of the front with the 1954 Pontiac grille. No mention of the car's color, engine, or interior. And no hint of this bayside scene, the lovely young lady in bathing suit and high heels, nor why she might be tugging on that tied-off rope. Who cares? It's a wonderful 1950s photo, and now you get to enjoy it.

---

changing fads and crazes in the late 1950s to the early 1960s as the baby-boomers became teenagers.

Yes, there were some bubble-top creations in the magazines and at shows, but the line between custom and rod blurred quickly as far as these were concerned. Just as quickly these morphed into rolling outhouses or bathtubs with twin-blown engines at car shows while drag racing and muscle cars took over the magazines. Custom cars that looked like the ones in this chapter simply vanished for more than two decades. Thankfully they're back, stronger than ever, a healthy part of today's

Chapter Nine *1950s Customs in Color*

rod and custom mix. More amazing is how many of these long-gone originals have been discovered and restored.

For now, let's relish what might delightfully be described as the decadence of the 1950s custom era. The photos I'm showing here are just a small sample from my collection. Obviously, I've left out many of the more famous cars to let you see images that are fresher and less familiar. You'll see a few examples of over-customizing or incipient show machines, but nothing like those in Chapter Seven. As I've said throughout this book, I think these photos are just as wonderful as the cars they depict. They're arty, opulent, trendy, and campy. So rather than ending with any sort of requiem, let's enjoy this last bounty of fabulous 1950s color like the crescendo at the end of a lively symphony. On with the show. More to come. Plenty more.

Dave Bugarin's Barris-built 1951 Mercury is one of those first famous few, and one about which little is known today, and it doesn't seem to have many fans. While the rolled-under hoodlip might be questionable, I love the 1953 Buick headlights, the grille, the hardtop roofline, and especially the frenched 1954 Packard taillights. Also note it has thinner 1954 Buick side chrome. When it debuted on the cover of the July 1955 *Car Craft*, it was shown in a sapphire blue and metallic gray; however, in the aged transparencies I have it's very difficult to tell if the near-black color is blue or green. I'd guess the interior is by Gaylord, but only the trunk is shown in the magazine. Rumors of this car being sighted in San Pedro neighborhoods have persisted for years.

Hot Rod Gallery 177

It has a Sheiks plaque on the front, but it doesn't have a Barris crest on the side so I don't know who did the slight (front only) top chop and other tasty custom work on Vince Villoa's 1951 Chevy fastback. But I do have a couple of other photos Barris took of the Hirohata Merc in front of the same house. As far as I know, this one never appeared in a magazine, and on the old film the color looks like a deep purple, but I'm not sure. Have you noticed yet that this is a four-door? The 1949–1951 Chevy fastback four-doors are the coolest ones to customize.

As you have seen, Valley Custom had sectioned a few earlier "fat fender" models. They sliced a piece out of the lower half of Ron Dunn's near-new slab-sided 1950 Ford coupe, and raised and opened the wheel wells to match in a sporty fashion. This became the shop's hallmark, followed by a 1950 Olds, the *Polynesian*. Other than shaving chrome, frenching the headlights, and making custom vertical taillights, this car was plenty radical as-is, introducing a more modern custom style. Few knew it had a flathead six engine. Later wrecked and re-done by Valley, it exists today in a well-weathered state.

178 Chapter Nine *1950s Customs in Color*

This 1951 Chevy mild-custom convertible appears to be painted the popular Glade Green metallic with beige/tan pleated interior. Again, this one didn't make the mags, so all I can tell you is the driver is Tom Charter and the car has 1955 Oregon plates plus a Kustoms plaque. The high-angle photo of the top-down convertible is what makes this a cool shot.

"The high-angle photo of the top-down convertible is what makes this a cool shot."

While most folks remember photos of Larry Watson's girlfriend Elaine Sterling posing beside *The Grapevine* 1950 Chevy in a gold lamé bathing suit, she looks surprisingly younger in photos taken by friend Lowell Helms a year earlier (1956). This is the second version of the car. Watson was of course the originator of wild, sinuous flames and scallops, but what's of note is that even by 1957 his own car was still painted in deep, luscious metallic colors, albeit two-tone, but with no scallops . . . yet.

Hot Rod Gallery 179

The reason this photo is a bit blurry is because rodder Tom Prufer took it with his Kodak at a drag strip in Tucson, Arizona, sometime in 1958 or 1959. This is one of the original famous chopped Mercs, built and owned by part-time Barris metal-man Frank Sonzogni. By this time he had sold it to a new owner who was racing it at the drags. I was surprised to see this car about five years ago, painted white with a Chrysler 392 Hemi engine. Then-owner Larry Dames of Tucson said he found and rescued it from a local wrecking yard.

"This impromptu, windblown setting couldn't have been staged to look any better."

I thought I didn't have a color photo of the excellent *Cocoa Rust* Buster Litton hardtop chopped 1950 Ford, but then I discovered this wonderful color transparency. I have no idea who the lady in the nice dress and high heels is, why she was taking a photo of the car with her own 35-mm camera, or who the photographer was who interrupted her. This impromptu, slightly windblown setting couldn't have been staged to look any better. Her hair nearly matches the color of the car.

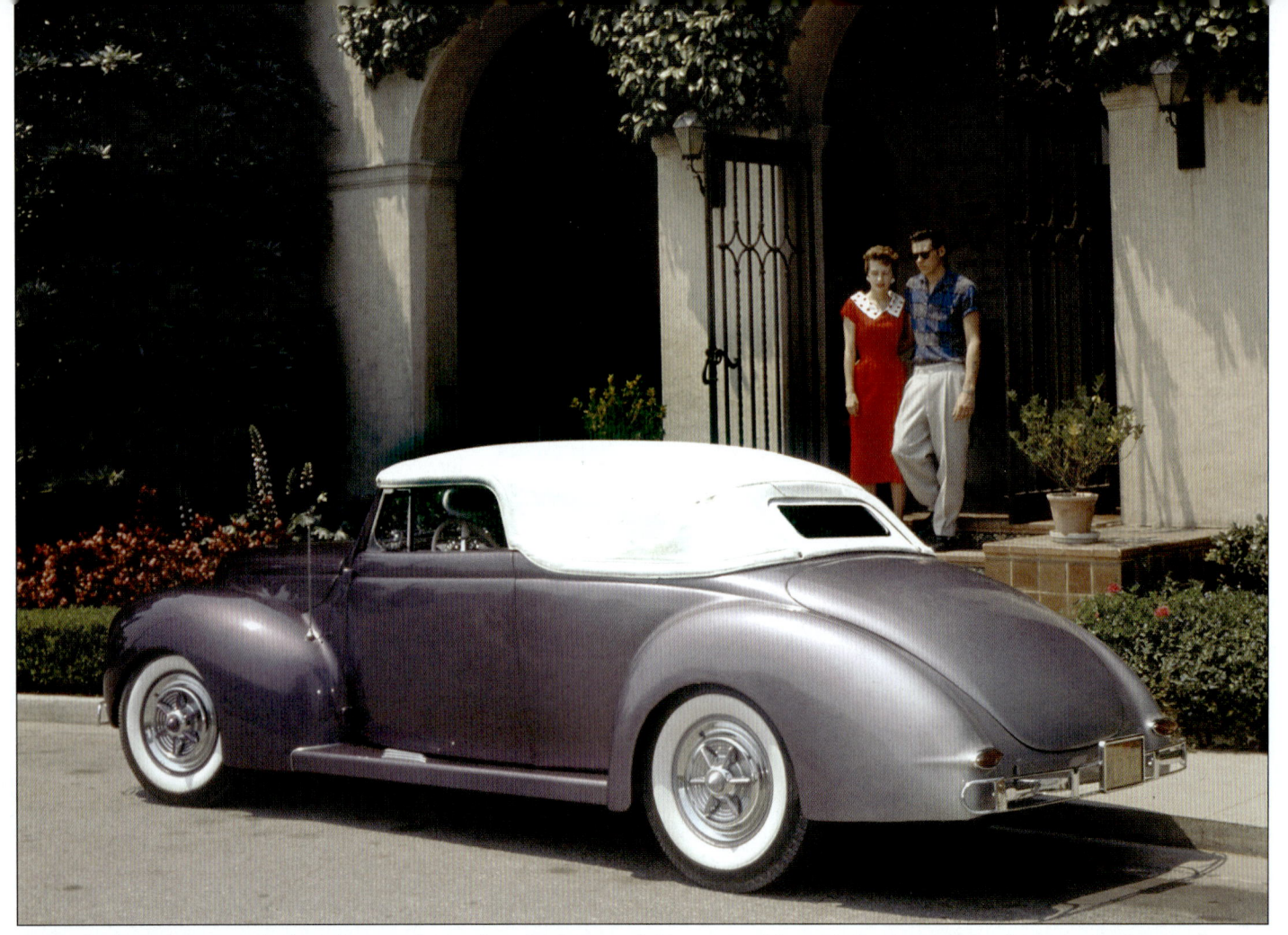

The only thing wrong with this photo is that it does look staged. However, Martin Woody, with his flattop, shades, and rolled shirtsleeves couldn't have looked much cooler. What's hard to notice in any pictures of it is the fade in the paint on his chopped Forty convertible. One 1958 magazine says, "Unusual color finish is reddish lavender lacquer," without ascribing credit to a painter. Actually, the color blends from a darker purple at the front to the lavender you see at the rear, possibly the first instance of this type of custom paint.

You saw a somewhat similar chopped 1950 Ford in a similar pose in front of a mid-century modern building on page 9, but don't be confused. This is Bob Dofflow's 1949 sedan; it was chopped and painted Titian Red and Alpine White by Don "The Bear" Roberts in his shop in Inglewood, California, in 1956. The grille is made from 1954 Ford parts; note the scoops with chrome teeth above the frenched headlights. I like the way the white lines on the pavement echo the angles of the building behind the car.

Hot Rod Gallery 181

Bill Gaylord's custom upholstery shop, just down the road from the Barris shop, did tons of tuck-and-roll on custom cars and ski boats; they also had cool customized shop trucks and other vehicles over the years. Probably the best of Bill's personal customs was this 1953 Olds 98 that he bought as a burned-out shell, cut the top off, and turned into this red and white, pleated and rolled showpiece, in part to demonstrate and advertise his own talents. I'm not sure who did the custom bodywork, including the chopped windshield and the complete Packard taillights in extended rear fenders, but the lift-off, padded top with the cantilevered rear-window opening was Gaylord's own hallmark work.

182 Chapter Nine *1950s Customs in Color*

The Gaylord interior in Jay Johnston's 1949 Ford is a tour de force, with pink rolls in the headliner, sun visors, and firewall, as well as the trunk. Also note the completely chromed 1951 dash. The story goes that he totaled a near-new 1949 Ford, then rebuilt and customized it with the help of Bill Bowman, using a much-chopped 1951 Victoria hardtop as well as a much-chromed 1951 Merc engine and auto trans. The addition of the bare-foot, bathing-suited girlfriend was hardly necessary, but it makes for a quintessentially campy 1950s photo. Why he changed to the darker purple/silver colors with original side trim (on page 9) is unknown; maybe it was typical updating.

When it comes to 1950s Buicks, the less customizing done, the better. In fact, these were truly the first factory customs, starting with the 1940s fastbacks. What's really amazing about Bob Paladino's 1957 with the three-piece back window is that he bought it brand new and drove it directly to Joe Bailon's NorCal shop. Joe dechromed it, frenched the twin 1956 taillight lenses into the rear fenders, reworked the headlights, and molded a lip over the stock grille. Then he sprayed it in his famous candy apple red lacquer over a gold base, taping off small bands of gold as accents. This was all done when it was a brand-new car!

Tom Liechty was a "car show guy" from Michigan who was first and best known for this extremely low, somewhat outlandish 1954 Chevy hardtop known as the *Copper Penny*. George Barris took the photos. I know it was in some of the small Eastern magazines, but I don't have them, so I can't offer further info, such as who did the work on the car. The huge bubble skirts were a regional custom trend of the time. The roof upholstery and fur trim were pure Liechty. The side pipes weren't attached to the car; they just lay on the ground once the car was in position. I won't say this was a typical Eastern custom (more a typical show car), but consider that Duane Steck's *Moonglow* was the same model, with a similar roof chop, from the same era.

Chapter Nine *1950s Customs in Color*

Saint Vasques was a member of the Renegades of Long Beach car club, along with Larry Watson, Duane Steck, and so many other well-known names. Saint's chopped Titian Red 1950 Chevy convertible was highly modified: molded 1953 grille shell, 1955 DeSoto grille, Cadillac headlights, Packard taillights, Olds windshield, etc. I found it in only one magazine and that gave no credit for bodywork, paint, or upholstery. It had a white lift-off top with a 1953 Bel Air rear window looks like a Gaylord. I like this angle, and this photo, best with the top off, the jutting tailfins, the glass-smooth paint, and the big smiles on the casual couple.

I'm including this photo because it's a neat mid-1950s urban scene. I'm not sure what these corner shopping areas were called, but they were precursors to the "mini mall" (and they still exist all over Los Angeles). The mild custom 1952 Merc is a bit of a puzzle. I have it listed as belonging to Tom Jefferies. I know it was the subject of a six-part "Building a Custom" series by Barris in *Car Craft* in mid-1955, where he calls it *The Japan* and the owner is Nobby Miyakawa. The colors are Golden Bronze Metallic over Copper Rust Metallic. And it's a cool photo.

Here's a perfect example of the genesis and mutation of a 1950s custom car. According to a small feature in the April 1959 *Custom Cars* magazine, Toby Halicki "used his own custom shop" in Gardena, California, to build his 1956 Buick. This first version, with a tube grille, double taillights, and dechroming, has what I consider the best scallop job (over candy red) ever applied on a custom car. It continues on the roof and trunk. The white wheel wells, flipper caps, and medium whitewalls were trends of the time.

> "This first version, with a tube grille, double taillights, and dechroming, has what I consider the best scallop job (over candy red) ever applied on a custom car."

The major redo to collect more of those trophies for the next season (quad headlights, pancaked hood, mouthy grille with a 1957 DeSoto bumper, and *no* scallops) can't be considered an improvement in looks. Halicki went on to make the very low budget/very high profit *Gone in 60 Seconds* movie; it was supposedly based on his own experiences.

186 Chapter Nine *1950s Customs in Color*

These photos aren't exactly in chronological order, but you'll notice trends changing. Barris had built this blue, chopped, skirted, and lightly scalloped 1940 Ford custom coupe for Tom Hocker of Oakland, California, a few years earlier, but this is the updated version with the "new look for 1958: quad headlights." However (and a bit surprisingly), he has retained vestiges of the earlier style, including the skirted, tail-dragging stance, spotlights, and wide whites with custom wheel covers. The late Ed Hegerty began restoring the car to this form, and his son is now continuing the project.

This is, hands down, my favorite shoebox Ford, starting with the unchopped coupe top. I love the lime green/gold lacquer, the canted quad headlights, the Chrysler grille, the split Pontiac bumpers, the side trim, the wheel coves, and even the 1957 Plymouth pointy hubcaps. About the only item I'd erase are the vestigial spotlights. Did you notice the curved, one-piece 1954 windshield? This is a fine example of the taste, subtlety, and cohesiveness of custom genius Gene Winfield during this period. This was actually a "second version" of LeRoy Goulart's 1950 Ford, which incorporated the headlights, coves, and windshield.

Hot Rod Gallery   187

"I'm a sucker for Tommy the Greek teardrops and pinstriping."

Here's an unusual, posterior view of Joe Bailon's *Candy Bird* that you very likely haven't seen before, and it makes a striking photo. It emphasizes Joe's hallmark candy apple red paint with gold highlights, not to mention his chrome-tube bumpers, big bullet exhaust outlets, and those zany rear fenders with upside-down Lincoln taillights that only Joe could imagine. I'm a sucker for Tommy the Greek teardrops and pinstriping, which are also a focal point of this picture.

This looks like a quintessential George Barris photo to me. It's certainly a quintessential Barris custom of the latter 1950s or early 1960s, and it's another "second version" that George named *The Modern Grecian*. He even did a how-to story on making those jet-age finned-aluminum wheel covers with the plastic thingies in the middle. But I would assume this particular photo was for a *Custom Grilles!* cover or even one of his many Spotlite Books on grilles, headlights, or some such. Believe it or not, this started as a 1948 Studebaker four-door. The interior was even wilder, with four bucket seats that swiveled around a TV set. What I love best about this photo, however, is the pearl yellow paint, which is complemented surprisingly well by the green candy accents, and the young lady's matching top.

Chapter Nine *1950s Customs in Color*

Louie Gaulrapp's mild-custom, lime green 1954 Chevy Bel Air is nice with a molded-in 1955 Ford grille, peaked hood with rounded corners, unusual shaded and frenched headlights, and louvers in both the hood and skirts. It's the summer of 1957 in SoCal, and nonchalant Louie looks the part leaning on the roof. I couldn't remember exactly why I chose this photo until I noticed them: the fuzzy dice! Thankfully they're not as pervasive now as they were ten to twenty years ago when customs were making their comeback, but I'm pretty sure this is the only custom from the 1950s in which I've actually seen a pair of big, fuzzy dice hanging from the rearview mirror. I don't even know where he got them.

In my recent book *Lost Hot Rods II* I wrote, "The semi-custom 1952 Mercury convertible he built for Jim Doyle of San Jose in 1959 isn't one of my favorite Bailon builds, but it did exactly what it was supposed to do. It created plenty of attention, got on several magazine covers, and won plenty of show trophies." Six covers in 1959 alone, to be exact. To see how it was abandoned on a Sacramento River levee in the 1970s, and then fully restored by Butch Gardner, get that book. But the reason I show this photo of the candy red convertible's better-looking backside is because of the period-perfect background. Not only do you have the roof of the aqua motel pool cabana with big coral-colored doors, but you have real palms and angled white beams over the pool itself, trumped by the whole wall painted with the lush tropical scene. This was 1959, long before wall murals were common.

I like this profile shot of Agie Winn's 1956 Mercury because it shows how these latter-1950s hardtop models needed far less customizing to look good. The 1956 Packard taillights and Cadillac rear bumper are the major mods, along with 1956 Buick side trim disappearing into a significantly reworked side scoop. Remember, this was all near-new stuff when this car was built.

> "These latter-1950s hardtop models needed far less customizing to look good."

Ray Kress' lime gold version of the 1956 Merc hardtop is tasty indeed. Built in 1958 by lesser-known Riley's Custom Shop in NorCal, it incorporates 1956 Packard taillights and Cadillac bumper guards with a sculpted rolled pan. The side scoops are mildly reworked to accept 1957 Ford side trim. The turnpike cruiser skirts and "kickstand" lakes pipes reflect earlier 1950s styles, while the chrome reversed rims and medium whitewalls are modern. And, of course, the streamlined hardtop needs no chopping. This car was just two years old when all this was done.

Chapter Nine *1950s Customs in Color*

I showed you the tail end of *Scoopy Doo* in black-and-white at the end of Chapter Five. Here's what the whole thing looked like in brilliant Bailon candy apple red, seen from an unusually high angle. Scoops, scallops, chrome bars, chrome teeth, chrome pipes, chrome wheels; this car had it all and then some. The "overhang" white pearl roof wasn't removable. It was just another of Joe's wild design ideas. This one was built to sit on angel hair and win big trophies.

You notice that lime green or lime gold was a popular custom color in the late 1950s. For some reason this is the only photo I have of the famous *R&C* "Dream Truck" in its final paint scheme before its fatal crash in fall 1958. I called Spence Murray to confirm that Barris did this lime gold with purple scallops paint job sometime in late 1957 or early 1958. I can tell that George took this photo, because that's the Lynwood City Hall in the background, one of his three favorite photo locations.

> "The 'overhang' white pearl roof wasn't removable. It was just another of Joe's wild design ideas. This one was built to sit on angel hair and win big trophies."

How could I say good-bye to the 1950s without a poolside custom car photo like this? Magazine copy would lead us to believe this pseudo-Polynesian setting is at a Balboa Beach resort, but cattle in the field across the way belie this. You can see that Frank Williams' 1952 Chevy coupe has a molded-in 1953 grille and a 1950 Olds one-piece windshield. Bodywork is credited to Miller's shop of Pasadena, as are fifteen coats each of Iridescent Plum and lavender lacquer. No credit is given for copious white tuck-and-roll, which includes not only the seat, but also a tarp over the back, and the steering wheel, and complete engine and trunk compartment covers that snap into place for car shows.

That's it. I hope seeing these photos has been as much fun for you as going through my collection and selecting them has been for me. Every picture tells a story, don't it?

Additional books that may interest you...

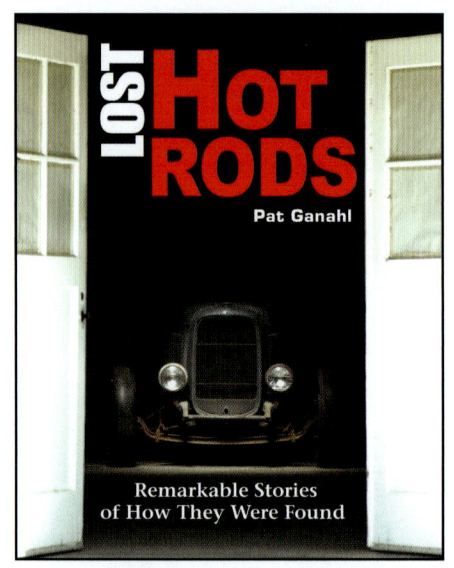

LOST HOT RODS *by Pat Ganahl* Author Pat Ganahl attempts to answer the questions about whatever happened to some of the great, legendary cars. Nearly all of these vintage rods and customs were found in urban or suburban garages—possibly right in your neighborhood—where they were parked years ago, maybe to save, perhaps torn apart for a rebuild, or in many cases they are projects that were started years ago and just never finished. The condition of such finds ranges from musty piles of parts, to dusty and cobwebbed originals, to pristine, still-show-quality beauties. Vintage and modern photography combine to make this book a must-have for hot rod enthusiasts and archeologists. Softbound, 8.5 x 11 inches, 192 pages, 200 color & 100 b/w photos. **Item # CT487**

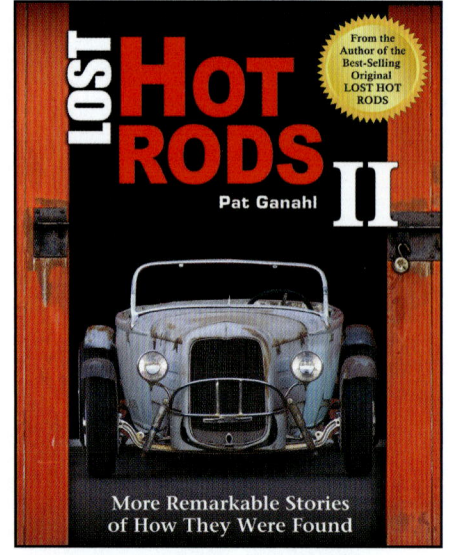

LOST HOT RODS II: More Remarkable Stories of How They Were Found *by Pat Ganahl* As a follow-up to the success of the original *Lost Hot Rods,* this book continues the fun of discovering whatever happened to many of the great rods and customs built in the early days of the sport. *Lost Hot Rods II* shares the full story of each car, including how it was originally built, when it dropped off the radar, and how it was ultimately found. Photos from the past and present are included to showcase the story behind each of these great cars. A perfect companion to the best-selling *Lost Hot Rods: Remarkable Stories of How They Were Found.* Hardbound, 8.5 x 11 inches, 192 pages. 450 color photos. **Item # CT506**

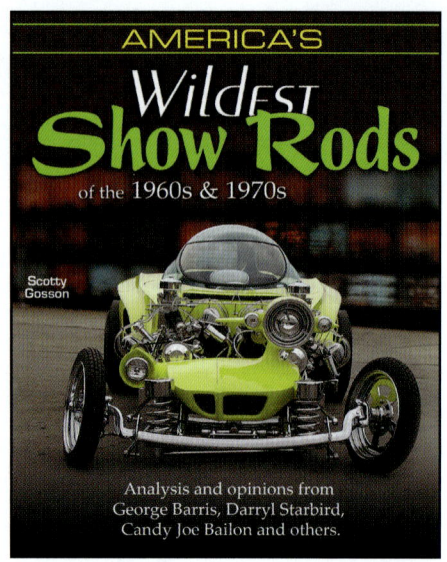

AMERICA'S WILDEST SHOW RODS OF THE 1960s & 1970s *by Scotty Gosson* In the 1960s and 1970s, a new breed of car was developed—the show rod. What began as visions of futuristic cars eventually morphed into cartoon-like representations of cars. This book features iconic cars from builders such as George Barris, Ed "Big Daddy" Roth, Gene Winfield, Dean Jeffries, "Candy" Joe Bailon, Bob Reisner, Darryl Starbird, and Tom Daniel—all important characters in promoting, designing, and building these insane pieces of rolling artwork. This unique book is a round-table discussion featuring all of these great customizers discussing the era, their builds, and each others' rods. Softbound, 8.5 x 11 inches, 160 pages, 300 color photos. **Item # CT510**

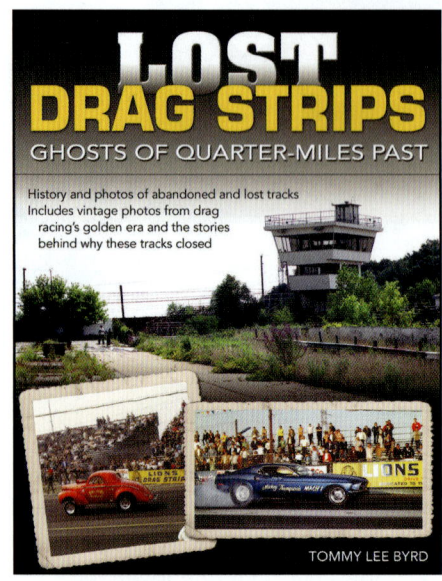

LOST DRAG STRIPS: Ghosts of Quarter-Miles Past *by Tommy Lee Byrd* This book takes a look at many of the lost quarter-mile tracks across the country. Some of them are gone completely, paved over to make room for housing developments or strip malls. Others are ghostly remnants of what once was, offering a sad and even eerie subject for the photographer. The images are teamed with vintage shots of drag racing's glory days, sharing what once was one of America's most popular pastimes with the modern reality facing these facilities today. For fans of drag racing's past, it's a sobering and interesting study. Softbound, 8.5 x 11 inches, 160 pages, 315 color and b&w photos. **Item # CT514**

Check out our website:
CarTechBooks.com

✓ **Find our newest books before anyone else**

✓ **Get weekly tech tips from our experts**

✓ **Get your ride or project featured on our homepage!**

Exclusive Promotions and Giveaways on Facebook
Like us to WIN! Facebook.com/CarTechBooks

www.cartechbooks.com or 1-800-551-4754

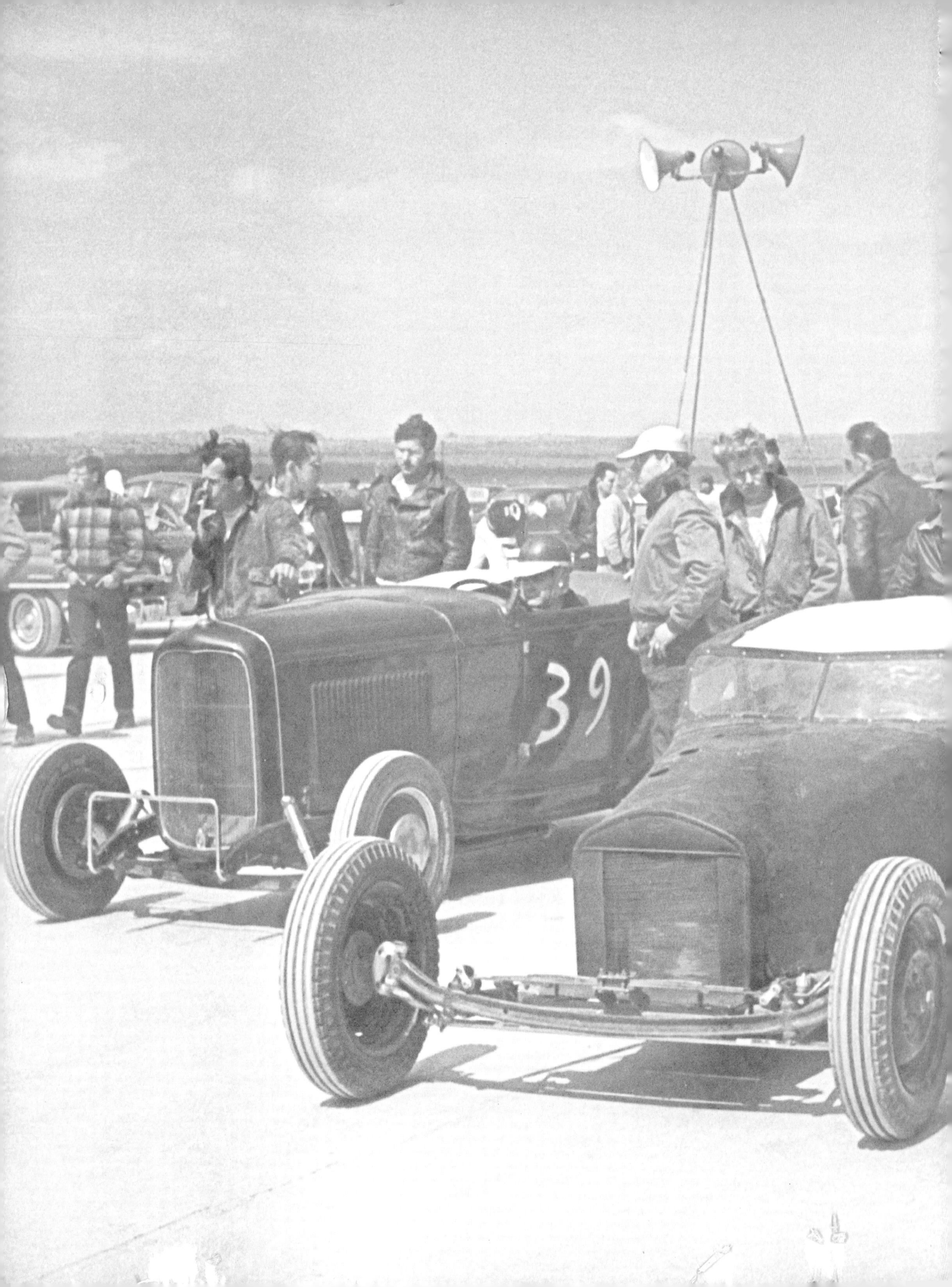